500 RECIPES
FOR WORKING WIVES

by Marguerite Patten

HAMLYN

LONDON · NEW YORK · SYDNEY · TORONTO

Cover photograph by Paul Williams

Published by The Hamlyn Publishing Group Limited
London · New York · Sydney · Toronto
Astronaut House, Feltham, Middlesex, England

Tenth impression 1981

ISBN 0 600 39227 9

Printed and bound in Great Britain by
Morrison & Gibb Ltd., London and Edinburgh

Contents

Introduction

This book has been written for the many housewives of today who run a home and have a part or full-time occupation as well. Often this brings more money for the family, but it does mean that the housewife has considerably less leisure and her housework, shopping and catering need to be planned carefully to avoid unnecessary fatigue.

Today many new appliances and convenience foods help towards easier preparation of meals, and chapters dealing with these precede the recipes, together with suggestions for 'bulk cooking' and wise menu planning. With the various menus you will find shopping reminders too, which will, I hope, make shopping quicker for you.

I hope you will find this book both helpful and enjoyable and it will give you new practical ideas for family meals.

MARGUERITE PATTEN.

Some Useful Facts and Figures

Notes on metrication

In case you wish to convert quantities into metric measures, the following tables give a comparison.

Solid measures

Ounces	Approx. grams to nearest whole figure	Recommended conversion to nearest unit of 25
1	28	25
2	57	50
3	85	75
4	113	100
5	142	150
6	170	175
7	198	200
8	227	225
9	255	250
10	283	275
11	312	300
12	340	350
13	368	375
14	396	400
15	425	425
16 (1 lb)	454	450
17	482	475
18	510	500
19	539	550
20 ($1\frac{1}{4}$ lb)	567	575

Note: When converting quantities over 20 oz first add the appropriate figures in the centre column, then adjust to the nearest unit of 25. As a general guide, 1 kg (1000 g) equals 2·2 lb or about 2 lb 3 oz. This method of conversion gives good results in nearly all cases, although in certain pastry and cake recipes a more accurate conversion is necessary to produce a balanced recipe.

Liquid measures

Imperial	Approx. millilitres to nearest whole figure	Recommended millilitres
$\frac{1}{4}$ pint	142	150
$\frac{1}{2}$ pint	283	300
$\frac{3}{4}$ pint	425	450
1 pint	567	600
$1\frac{1}{2}$ pints	851	900
$1\frac{3}{4}$ pints	992	1000 (1 litre)

Oven temperatures

The table below gives recommended equivalents.

	°C	°F	Gas Mark
Very cool	110	225	$\frac{1}{4}$
	120	250	$\frac{1}{2}$
Cool	140	275	1
	150	300	2
Moderate	160	325	3
	180	350	4
Moderately hot	190	375	5
	200	400	6
Hot	220	425	7
	230	450	8
Very hot	240	475	9

Notes for American and Australian users

In America the 8-oz measuring cup is used. In Australia metric measures are now used in conjunction with the standard 250-ml measuring cup. The Imperial pint, used in Britain and Australia, is 20 fl oz, while the American pint is 16 fl. oz. It is important to remember that the Australian tablespoon differs from both the British and American tablespoons; the table below gives a comparison. The British standard tablespoon, which has been used throughout this book, holds 17·7 ml, the American 14·2 ml, and the Australian 20 ml. A teaspoon holds approximately 5 ml in all three countries.

Ready-prepared foods to help you

One of the ways to easy catering is to make use of the very large range of ready-prepared foods, which mean that meals may be cooked or presented with the minimum of time spent on them. Obviously convenience foods (as these are generally called) are often more expensive and therefore it is wise to try and use a combination of ready-prepared and fresh foods.

Modern convenience foods have been prepared so that the foods retain the maximum of flavour and food value. These are the types of convenience foods you may find:

Ready-prepared foods – bread, cakes, meat pies, fish cakes, etc. prepared by the individual shopkeeper

Accelerated freeze dried and dried foods – in the form of complete meals, soups, sauces and sauce mixes, etc.

Canned foods – of every kind

Frozen foods – of every kind

Soups: canned and dehydrated soups need no extra flavourings added, although canned or dried soups are made more interesting if you
a) add herbs to flavour
b) mix 2 well-chosen flavours together, i.e. chicken and asparagus, tomato and mixed vegetable, etc.
c) top with cream, or dilute with milk rather than water.

Hors d'oeuvre: often a somewhat 'frugal' meal can be turned into an interesting one if preceded by a good hors d'oeuvre.

Stock up with gherkins, cocktail onions, sardines, canned mixed vegetable salad, anchovies, roll-mop herrings and other canned fish.

Fish: canned *salmon* (pink – cheaper quality), makes a good meal as:
a) *Fish pie.* Flake the fish, put into a pie dish, top with sliced hard-boiled eggs, cheese or white sauce and creamed potatoes – then brown in the oven.
b) *Salmon fish cakes.* [F] see page 11. Mix about 8-10 oz. flaked salmon with the same amount of mashed potatoes (dehydrated potatoes are excellent). Bind with an egg, form into 8 round cakes. Coat in a little seasoned flour, a beaten egg, then crisp breadcrumbs, and fry in hot fat until crisp and brown (see also frozen fish cakes).

Red salmon is excellent in salads or part of an hors d'oeuvre or as a sandwich filling.

Tuna fish may be used in the same way.

Frozen fish may be purchased in various forms including ready-coated fish.

Frozen or ready-made Fish Cakes – cook as directed but to make them more interesting –
a) top with sliced cheese and melt under the grill
b) top or serve with a mushroom, tomato or cheese sauce
c) top with scrambled or fried egg.

Canned or frozen shrimps, prawns and other shellfish – excellent as an hors d'oeuvre or to put into salads, sauces, omelettes or pancakes. Always allow frozen shellfish to thaw out at room temperature before using, otherwise it is very tough.

Meat: Hamburgers or other frozen or ready-prepared meat cakes are more nutritious or interesting if:

a) topped with sliced cheese after cooking and heated for a few minutes under the grill;
b) topped with rolls of bacon and served with rings of pineapple;
c) topped with thick tomato purée.

Ready-cooked meats . . . here are a few types readily available:

Canned corned beef – to serve cold or in various hot dishes as the curried slices, page 50; barbecued beef, page 46; fritters, page 47; beef and tomato puffs, page 48.

Frankfurter sausages – heat in stock or the brine in the can. Use as ordinary sausages.

Cooked or canned ham – to serve cold; or this makes an excellent hot meal with either a Madeira sauce, page 79 or Cumberland sauce, page 79.

Canned kidneys – excellent if heated and served:

a) on toast as a quick snack;
b) as a filling for pancakes or omelettes, or sauce over hard-boiled eggs, see page 32;
c) heat and serve with grilled or fried bacon.

If you add 1-2 tablespoons port wine to the kidneys you will improve the flavour.

Canned luncheon meats of various kinds – to serve cold or as cooked ham or corned beef.

Salami – excellent in salads or serve as an hors d'oeuvre.

Salted brisket or silverside – to serve cold. Can be heated in stock for a hot meal (do not use very salt flavoured stock).

Canned stewed steak or *steak and vegetables* – these may be heated and served as a quick stew; various flavourings can be added – curry powder, paprika, herbs.

The steak can be used for a meat pie – top with pastry and heat until the pastry is crisp and brown, see page 73, use also as a filling for pancakes.

Cooked or canned tongue – remember you can buy small cans of calves' or lambs' tongues as well as ox tongue. Serve cold or heat in

a) mixed vegetable sauce, page 79;
b) Madeira sauce, page 79;
c) tomato sauce, page 79 or 81.

Vegetables: there is a wide range of prepared vegetables available:

Canned vegetables just need reheating.

Frozen vegetables should be cooked as instructions on the packet.

Accelerated freeze dried vegetables should be prepared as instructions on the packet.

The 'old fashioned' *dried peas, beans*, etc. should be soaked overnight in cold water then cooked steadily with seasoning until tender (this takes 2 hours approximately), so these cannot be regarded as time-saving.

To turn vegetables into a meal:

a) Buy canned or frozen mixed vegetables; heat or cook as instructions and serve in a cheese sauce;
b) Prepare vegetables as (a) and put as a filling in an omelette;
c) Prepare vegetables as (a), add to a cheese flavoured batter as a cheese and vegetable Yorkshire pudding – recipe see page 53;
d) Baked beans, which are an excellent protein food, are a general favourite and can be served on toast, as an accompaniment to cooked dishes, or in salads. They are also turned into quickly prepared light meals:

1 **Bacon and bean bake** . . . recipe page 57.
2 **Bean scramble** . . . tip the beans into a saucepan with a knob of butter, heat and then add several beaten eggs and scramble lightly. Serve on toast.
3 **Bean flan** . . . line a flan ring with uncooked pastry and cover with a layer of canned baked beans, then top with several beaten eggs, mixed with a little seasoning and grated cheese. Bake for approximately 10–15 minutes in the centre of a hot oven (425–450°F., Gas Mark 6–7) then lower the heat to moderate for a further 20–25 minutes until the pastry is brown and the filling firm; serve hot or cold.

Ready-prepared rice and pasta

Rice: Creamed rice is one of the most popular prepared desserts; to use this you can:

a) put it into a pie dish and heat for a short time in the oven;
b) put it into a serving dish, top with drained canned, or cooked, frozen or fresh fruit then cover with a glaze made of 2–3 tablespoons heated redcurrant or apple jelly, diluted with a little water. This is called a Fruit Condé (the name depending on fruit used).

Spaghetti: Although there are other types of prepared pasta, spaghetti in tomato or tomato and cheese sauce is the most popular. It can be served on toast, heated and served as an accompaniment to cooked dishes or used in place of cooked pasta in pasta dishes, see page 80.

If using canned spaghetti in tomato sauce as the basis for a complete meal, remember it should be topped with an egg, cheese, bacon or other protein food.

Ready-prepared cakes, sponges, sponge flans

In supermarkets, grocers and cake shops there is a wide variety of prepared cakes; most of these can be served as they are, but you will find plain sponge cakes that form the basis of rather more interesting gâteaux if they are 'dressed up' (see below).

Sponge flan cases are also available and these can be filled in a variety of ways:

a) fill with ice cream and top with a quick chocolate sauce . . . to make this, break up about 4 oz. plain chocolate, put it into a basin with 2 tablespoons water and heat over very hot water until melted;

b) fill with well-drained fruit . . . a more professional look is given if the fruit is topped with a glaze;
   easy glaze: put 3 tablespoons redcurrant jelly (or use sieved apricot jam with light coloured fruit) into a saucepan, add about 6 tablespoons syrup from the cooked or canned fruit or water and sugar to taste, plus a squeeze of lemon juice. Heat until the jelly melts, then cool slightly and brush over the fruit;

c) make an ordinary 1 pint jelly, but use only $\frac{3}{4}$ pint water; when nearly set whisk in $\frac{1}{4}$ pint thin cream and spoon into the sponge flan case. When the jelly is firm top with well-drained fruit.

5 ways to dress up a sponge cake

It is possible to turn a ready-made or home-made sponge cake into quite a decorative gâteau with very little effort.

Apricot and almond gâteau

Blanch 2–4 oz. almonds. To do this put them into boiling water for approximately 1 minute. Lift out and remove the skins. Dry on kitchen paper, then split the almonds. (This is often called 'flaking'. You can buy packets of commercially flaked almonds which are in much finer slices.) Put the almonds on a baking tray and either brown under a low grill or for a short time in the oven.

Split a sponge cake, sandwich with apricot jam, spread the sides with apricot jam and coat in the almonds as method given under the coconut raspberry gâteau. Spread the apricot jam on top and top with the split almonds.

Coconut raspberry gâteau

Split a sponge cake, if this has not been done, and sandwich with jam and desiccated coconut. (If you buy a sponge cake already filled with jam, separate carefully and sprinkle with coconut.) Then put the cake together again. Spread the sides of the cake with raspberry jam, putting approximately 1 oz. desiccated coconut on to a sheet of greaseproof paper, hold the cake rather like a hoop and roll over the coconut so that it adheres to the jam. Turn the cake with the top uppermost, spread with raspberry jam and cover with desiccated coconut. Decorate the top with halved glacé cherries if wished.

Chocolate gâteau

Put 4 oz. plain chocolate broken in small pieces into a basin over hot but *not boiling* water. Heat until the chocolate is melted, then blend half of this with 1 oz. butter and 1 oz. icing sugar. Split the cake and sandwich with this chocolate filling. Put the cake together again and spread thinly with the remaining melted chocolate. This is sufficient for a 6-inch sponge.

Fruit gâteau

Split a sponge and sandwich with whipped cream and fresh fruit, or well-drained canned or defrosted frozen fruit. Put the cake together and top with whipped cream and more fruit. You need at least $\frac{1}{4}$ pint of thick cream and a large packet of frozen fruit, a large can of fruit or 8–12 oz. fresh fruit for a 6–7-inch sponge.

Fudge and walnut gâteau

Buy a $\frac{1}{4}$ lb. vanilla or other flavoured fudge (but not one containing nuts). Put the fudge in a basin over hot water with 1 tablespoon of cream from the top of the milk, or thin cream. Heat gently until a fairly sticky mixture. Beat to bind the cream and fudge, spread over the top of the cake and decorate with halved walnuts. The amount of fudge gives a generous topping to a 7-inch sponge.

Ready-prepared pastry
Frozen pastry is of excellent quality and can be used in any recipe where fresh pastry is mentioned.

Remember when a recipe says 8 oz. pastry it means pastry made with 8 oz. flour, etc. **NOT** 8 oz. complete weight – so when buying frozen pastry you must take this into account. *8 oz. puff pastry* in a recipe refers to pastry made with 8 oz. flour, 8 oz. butter, etc. and this means *you must buy* 1 *lb. frozen puff pastry*.

8 oz. short crust, on the other hand, refers to pastry made with 8 oz. flour, 4 oz. fat, etc. and you need to use only 12 *oz. frozen short crust*.

Packets of *pastry mixes* should be handled according to directions and the weight calculated accordingly.

Ready-prepared puddings
There are so many different types of prepared foods for puddings:

Canned puddings . . . heat as directed and take care how you open the can when the pudding is hot. Serve with quick and easy sauces, see page 53.

Packets of pudding mixes, e.g. crumbles, etc. Try these as directed; you will often find they can be improved by adding a little extra flavouring to the fruits, etc.

Canned fruits to serve from the can or to be used in easy desserts; many are given in this book.

Frozen fruits – defrost as directed.

Ice cream, which makes an easy dessert by itself, or to serve in quick puddings, see page 87.

Appliances to help you

When you have very little time to spend in running a home, modern labour-saving appliances are a wise investment. Here are some of the appliances relating to cooking which should be considered.

AUTOMATIC COOKERS
Today anyone buying either an electric or gas cooker will have an automatic timing device incorporated. Directions for using the cookers will be given by the manufacturers, but when considering the value of these cookers remember:

Advantages
a) You may put dishes (or complete meals) into the cold oven and set the controls so that the oven switches on automatically at a pre-planned time. This will enable you to come home in the evening and find a meal ready-cooked, or to put breakfast in the oven overnight;

b) You may put food into the oven, switch on or light the oven, then go out and the oven will automatically switch off, so food will not be over-cooked.

Disadvantages or problems in using automatic cookers
a) One needs to place the food carefully to make certain *all* dishes are well-cooked at the same time.

Very few recipes are unsuitable for putting in a cold oven – for greater details see comments under some of menus.

b) It is unwise to have uncooked food standing in a closed oven for any length of time during very hot weather.

How to use an automatic oven
1 Select the menu – choose dishes that need approximately the same cooking time.

2 Place the prepared dishes in the correct position in the oven, i.e. those that need the hottest part of the oven towards the top of the oven, etc.

3 If you are afraid of the pudding or pie becoming too brown by the time the meat, etc.

is cooked, put a double sheet of greaseproof paper or foil on top to hinder browning.

You can adjust cooking times slightly by the position in which you place the food and by the container which you select, e.g. a sponge pudding that takes 1 hour in a 7-inch container would take $1\frac{1}{4}$ hours if cooked in a deep 6-inch container – so if necessary alter the size of the cooking container to suit your menu.

4 *Timing*: if you are sure you will be at home to take the food out of the oven the *moment* it is ready and the oven turns itself off, allow just 5–10 minutes extra cooking time for the oven heating-up period. If you *are not sure* you will be at home to take the food out of the oven the moment it is cooked, then allow only normal cooking time, for the food will continue to cook in the warm oven and warm containers, even though the gas or electricity is switched off.

5 *Remember* to put plates and dishes to warm, if possible in warming drawer.

Foods that can be put into a cold oven and left to cook automatically are many.

Meat, poultry, fish: cook as usual – do not over-time the cooking period for fish.

Vegetables: do *not* try and cook green vegetables this way.

Peas, carrots, other root vegetables: put into a casserole, cover with cold water, season, add small knob of butter or margarine. Cover with tightly fitting foil or paper, then a lid. Cook with the menu, adjust the size of potatoes, carrots, etc. according to the size of the joint of meat, or cooking time of the main dish.

Roast potatoes: potatoes discolour if left exposed to the air, so coat the potatoes in melted fat *before* they are put in the oven.

Pastry: short or flaky excellent; *not* suitable for puff pastry.

Cake and sponge mixtures: excellent, except for a sponge where the eggs and sugar are whisked together.

Yeast cookery: excellent; make sure that the dough is well proved and the oven set to switch on almost immediately the food is put into oven.

Batters: a Yorkshire pudding batter can be left in a *very well* greased tin in the oven.

MIXERS

There is a very wide range of electric mixers on the market today, ranging from hand whisks to larger models that incorporate a variety of attachments. Mention is made of a mixer or blender in some recipes.

Advantages

a) An electric mixer deals with the 'energetic' tasks of creaming, whisking, beating, without any physical effort on your part. If you buy a mixer complete with a stand and bowl, these jobs will be done automatically as you do not need to hold the mixer;

b) A blender (or liquidiser) will purée vegetables or fruits (almost taking the place of a sieve). It will prepare parsley, etc. for stuffings, 'chop' nuts, herbs and other ingredients.

Disadvantages or problems

a) One must learn to use the appliance carefully – over-beating of cake or sponge mixtures can cause a tough texture, etc.

b) A blender should have ingredients added carefully; over-filling often prevents the rotating blades at the base of the goblet from being effective.

REFRIGERATOR AND HOME FREEZER

Refrigerator

Models are obtainable in varying sizes to fit under working surfaces, into kitchen units, etc.

Advantages

a) Food is kept at the correct temperature for hygienic storage; perishable foods do not spoil – so you save money;

b) Time may be saved by shopping less frequently, preparing dishes in advance;

c) One can freeze ice cream mixture, etc., make ice, store frozen foods – the time depends upon the particular model.

Disadvantages or problems

a) Food will not keep indefinitely, only a limited time, so take care not to over-stock the cabinet with one type of food;

b) Unless foods are covered or stored according to the manufacturer's instructions they can become dry or lose flavour.

Home freezer

A home or deep freezer could be called an 'extension' of a refrigerator in that foods keep a great deal longer.

Advantages

a) One can buy in large quantities, saving time and often a considerable amount of money;

b) There can always be a large selection of food – ready-cooked or ready to cook – available;

c) One completely eliminates wastage of food.

Disadvantages or problems

a) Home freezers are large so space may be difficult – they can, however, be kept in garages;

b) One needs to package food carefully when freezing and use a sufficiently low temperature for good results – follow manufacturer's instructions;

c) While MOST foods can be frozen, some are less satisfactory than others and it is wise to follow any particular recommendation in manufacturer's books, etc. Dishes marked [F] in this book freeze very well, but *where a sauce, etc. is thickened with flour or cornflour* use cornflour if you intend to freeze the dish or a portion of it. This prevents the sauce becoming thin with storage.

In addition to the individual dishes given in this book the following guide as to some of the foods that freeze well may help you to determine the value of a home freezer in YOUR home.

Hors d'oeuvre

Smoked fish – salmon, trout, etc. Excellent.

Pâté – very good – the less creamy the pâté the better it freezes.

Grapefruit – cut away the skin (as one does an orange for orange salad), then cut away the fruit pulp from the skin, etc. Freeze either

without sugar or with a sprinkling of sugar. Excellent.

Melon – freeze in a lemon or ginger flavoured syrup, cut the pulp in balls or neatly dice.

All these items should be allowed to thaw out gradually before using.

Soups

Most soups freeze well, but vegetable purée soups, meat and poultry soups are particularly good. Simply tip the frozen soup into a pan to reheat.

Fish

Naturally commercially frozen fish can be kept in your home freezer, but it is *very important* that uncooked fish is stored in the home freezer *only* IF YOU ARE SURE IT IS VERY FRESHLY CAUGHT.

Made-up fish dishes such as fish pies, fish cakes, fish au gratin, etc., all freeze well, but do follow directions in the manufacturer's book as to the time for keeping, so that the flavour is unimpaired.

Most fish dishes may be taken from the home freezer and cooked from the frozen state.

Meat

Uncooked meat freezes perfectly – wrap well, as directed by the manufacturer. You may find a butcher is willing to allow you to buy large quantities of meat (and will joint this for you) at a cheaper price per lb. than when buying normal quantities.

Also many firms today offer specially cheap packs of meat products for users of home freezers. Small pieces of frozen meat, i.e. chops, steaks, rissoles, etc, may be cooked from the frozen state, but it is better to allow larger joints to thaw out before cooking.

All types of stews – curries, etc. – freeze well. Prepare and freeze, or prepare, cook and freeze. You may not want to keep casserole dishes themselves in the home freezer, so line the dish with foil before cooking and freezing. When the food is frozen until very firm you can then lift it from the casserole, and wrap as directed in your home freezer instructions. When ready to cook or reheat put back into casserole.

Meat pies and meat puddings (such as steak and kidney pudding) all freeze well. You can cook the pie, etc., lightly, then complete cooking when required.

Sauces

The only sauce that does not freeze at all is a mayonnaise.

You can freeze tomato sauce, ordinary cheese and other sauces if thickened with cornflour (although these keep only for a limited period of several weeks, and no longer).

A Hollandaise sauce is excellent, keeps well for several weeks also.

Vegetables

Larger quantities of commercially frozen vegetables can be purchased at cheaper rates, but it is possible to prepare and freeze many of your own vegetables – following the manufacturer's instructions for 'blanching' (i.e. boiling for a very short time) then cooling and packing.

Fruits

Many fruits can be frozen (either halved or whole) in a sugar and water syrup. Cook the fruit lightly in the syrup, to make it tender, but unbroken, then cool and freeze – most suitable are: halved plums, damsons, greengages, cooking cherries, apricots.

Freeze the ripe fruit with sugar to taste if wished – fruits frozen this way are: strawberries, raspberries, ripe gooseberries, blackcurrants, etc.

Freeze fruit purées to use in many ways; most useful fruits are: apples, damsons, apricots, etc.

Pastries and pies

Uncooked pastry freezes well – make or buy short, puff and flaky pastry. Defrost just enough to roll it out. Pies already prepared but not cooked can be frozen ready to cook when desired, or the pie may be baked lightly then reheated. Pastry cases (vol-au-vent, etc.) may be prepared and frozen or cooked and frozen UNFILLED.

Suet crust pastry for steak and kidney or fruit puddings also freezes well. I find it best to half-cook the pudding, so the crust is light and set,

then continue cooking when it is required. Choux pastry used for éclairs and cream buns must be cooked before freezing. The buns, etc., may be filled with whipped cream or a savoury filling before freezing.

Desserts

There are many desserts that freeze well – to give a few examples:

trifle topped with custard freezes well, but for a period of *only a few weeks;*

cold cream soufflés and fruit mousse freeze well for up to 2 months;

ice cream and water ices freeze excellently, and should be kept up to 2–3 months.

Recipes for these are given in the Planning a Party Section, beginning page 85.

Cakes, etc.

Many cakes freeze well, including light sponges (freeze with filling, or better still freeze flavoured butter icing separately) and cream and fruit or jam filled sponges are excellent. Bread, buns and scones all freeze well, and so do sandwiches, see page 83.

Complete meals

Many complete meals can be frozen on aluminium foil dishes, so that they may be reheated when required.

BULK BUYING OF FROZEN FOOD

Until recently a home freezer was considered 'almost a luxury', but during the last year or two people have realised that this will give increased leisure and, if used wisely, it will also save money – see page 11. The use of home freezers has developed so quickly that it is now possible for the housewife with a home freezer to buy larger quantities of frozen foods – vegetables, fish, ice cream, etc. – at considerably cheaper prices than those charged for the normal packs sold by retailers. These foods are cooked according to the instructions on the packet, and stored in the home freezer until needed.

Our cover picture illustrates dishes made with several favourite kinds of frozen foods. In addition, under this home freezer service you are offered a range of unusual complete dishes that just need heating.

PRESSURE COOKERS

Because the temperature inside a pressure cooker or pressure pan, as it may be called, is raised much higher than the usual cooking temperature *when the valve is in position*, foods cook more quickly than usual.

Advantages

a) You save a great deal of time in cooking;
b) Some foods (stewing meat, etc.) that tend to be tough when cooked by ordinary methods are much more tender when cooked under pressure.

Disadvantages or problems

a) Because accurate timing is so important in a pressure cooker, foods can be spoiled (green vegetables in particular) by even one minute over-cooking.

Foil, plastic containers, etc.

Once upon a time it was difficult to prepare food in advance without it becoming dry and unpleasant to eat or to see, but today there is such a wide range of containers, covers, etc., that food can be prepared when time is available.

Foil

Use foil for wrapping sandwiches; food in your refrigerator; food in the oven (to keep it clean), etc.

What are the drawbacks to using foil?

In storing there are none – the food keeps perfectly. In cooking food it takes longer as the heat must penetrate through the foil. Allow about 15 minutes longer cooking time when you have wrapped meat, etc. in foil, or if more convenient use the same cooking time but raise the heat of the oven 1 point in gas, and 25°F. with electricity.

Polythene bags

These are excellent for wrapping food in the refrigerator and will keep it very moist.

What are the drawbacks of polythene bags?

You do get some condensation, so that food that should be crisp becomes slightly softened –

this does not matter if it is being reheated.

Polythene boxes

These are probably some of the most useful of all coverings or containers, since the food is just placed into the box and covered. They keep the food from drying out in the refrigerator or larder.

What are the drawbacks of polythene boxes?

Most foods are very good if stored in very tightly covered containers, *but* cooked meat, uncooked meat and fish MUST have air circulation round them.

Smaller equipment to save you time

There are many smaller appliances that are invaluable from a time-saving point of view.

It is very difficult to select 'gadgets', for often an over-persuasive salesman can make one buy small appliances that sound wonderful, but save little if any time.

These are the kind of questions to ask oneself, therefore, when looking at this kind of equipment:

a) do I need this and how many times a week would I use it?
b) how easy will it be to put together and/or to wash up? Often 'gadgets' save time in use but take up so much time to clean that their value is lost.

Here are some small appliances that I find save me a great deal of precious time.

General time saving

A flat whisk – not only for whisking egg whites, if I do not want to use an electric mixer – but to keep sauces smooth with a quick whisk, rather than continual stirring.

For cutting

Good knives – bad knives take much longer to do the job – *you need:*

sharp vegetable knife for preparing vegetables and fruit – more than one is useful in case the family wish to help.

a cook's knife – for chopping, etc.

a flexible knife to fillet and bone fish – not essential if you have a friendly fishmonger.

a flat bladed palette knife for blending ingredients, lifting food from pans, etc.

In addition a *vegetable parer*, *bean slicer* (the latter is only good if you have really fresh firm beans).

kitchen scissors are invaluable for cutting rinds from bacon, chopping parsley, etc.

For grating, etc.

A good *grater* – there are various kinds – in some you rub the food (cheese, etc.) against the holes, in others you put the food into the container and turn the handle.

If you wish to shred lots of vegetables, such as potatoes for thin slices for frying, or cucumber for salads, the classic *French mandolin* is excellent – much cheaper versions are now available.

A *hand mincer* saves a great deal of time, for you can mince not only meat but onion, and other ingredients too – which is much quicker than chopping.

For extracting juice

A good *lemon squeezer* – when choosing see that the design is such that ONLY the juice will flow through – in some the holes are large enough for little bits of pulp to come through too.

These are just a few of the every day utensils that enable you to do 'day to day' jobs easily as well as quickly.

Making use of time

Time is one of the most precious commodities when you are busy, and there are many ways of using this wisely.

When making pastry:

Either prepare double or treble quantities, wrap the surplus and store for a few days in the refrigerator, or for weeks, in the home freezer. When making short crust, however, if you have no refrigerator, simply rub the fat into the flour and store the surplus in a screw-topped jar.

It is worthwhile cooking an extra pastry flan case, and either freezing this or putting it into an airtight tin, and reheating some days later.

When making a plain cake mixture:

When making a plain Victoria sandwich or economical fruit cake it may be possible to prepare an extra quantity and use the surplus as a steamed pudding.

When preparing a sauce:

Make double quantities of a white or similar sauce. Store the surplus carefully in the refrigerator and reheat 2–3 days later, whisking hard to make it smooth again.

Note: sauces made with cornflour instead of flour reheat rather better – use $\frac{1}{2}$ oz. cornflour in place of each 1 oz. flour.

When cooking fruit:

Prepare double quantities so that you may make quick desserts.

When cooking vegetables:

You can use left-over peas, beans, potatoes in salads, etc.

It is, however, a mistake to cook too large a quantity of green vegetables, for freshly cooked vegetables contain important vitamins for your family.

Planning menus ahead

Menus need to be planned with a regard to family tastes, wise nutrition and family budgets, but there are times when you can plan menus to save a great deal of time.

The following *three* menus are given as an illustration of this – they are designed to cover: **dinner** and **supper** or **lunch** on the first day, and **dinner** or **a main meal** on the second day; this would therefore make them suitable for a weekend, so giving yourself a little extra time.

Menu A
Dinner
Ham flan
Runner beans
Golden topped potatoes
Chocolate orange sundae

Menu B
Supper or Lunch
Cheese, egg and vegetable
pie with green salad
Malted fruit gâteau

Menu C
Dinner
Ham croquettes
Russian salad
Tomatoes
Walnut apple tart

All recipes serve 4.

WORKING PLAN

Make pastry with 10 oz. flour, pinch salt, 5 oz. fat, etc. for –
Menu A Ham flan – this uses approximately 6 oz. flour, etc.
Menu C Walnut apple tart – this uses approximately 4 oz. flour, etc.

Make 1¼ pints sauce for –
Menu B Cheese, egg and vegetable pie (¾ pint sauce)
Menu C Salad dressing for Russian salad (½ pint sauce)

Cook enough potatoes for –
Menus A, B and C.

Cook enough beans for –
Menus A and C.

Cook enough carrots for –
Menus B and C.

Hard-boil 6 eggs for –
Menu B Cheese, egg and vegetable pie (4 eggs)
Menu C Ham croquettes (2 eggs)

Make golden sponge mixture for –
Menus B and C.

General cooking plan
(This gives **Menu A** and preparations for **Menus B** and **C**)

Bake the Ham flan and Walnut apple tart
Bake the Malted fruit gâteau
Boil vegetables
Hard-boil eggs

Before Menu B is served:
brown the Cheese, egg and vegetable pie

Before Menu C is served:
cook the Ham croquettes

Menu A

Ham flan [F] : line an 8-inch flan ring, or tin, with short crust pastry. Bake the flan 'blind', i.e. without a filling, for 10 minutes in a hot oven (425–450°F., Gas Mark 6–7). To keep the flan a good shape line with greased greaseproof paper and crusts of bread or haricot beans. Meanwhile, whisk ½ pint milk into 2 beaten eggs, add 8 oz. chopped cooked ham, 1 tablespoon chopped spring onion and seasoning. Remove the paper, crusts etc., from the flan case, spoon in the ham mixture and return to the oven, lowering the heat to moderate (350–375°F., Gas Mark 4–5), leave for approximately 40 minutes, or until the filling is set. Serve hot or cold.

Runner beans: cook amount required for this meal PLUS 8–12 oz. for salad, **Menu C.**

Golden topped potatoes: boil sufficient potatoes for this meal PLUS approximately 12 oz. for the pie, **Menu B,** and 8 oz. for salad, **Menu C.** Drain the potatoes, put those required for the meal into an ovenproof dish topped with a little melted butter or margarine. Sprinkle crisp crumbs over the potatoes and put into the oven for a few minutes. Add a little chopped parsley before serving.

Chocolate orange sundae: make chocolate sauce: put 2 oz. butter or margarine, 1 tablespoon golden syrup, 2 oz. drinking chocolate and 3 tablespoons water into a saucepan. Heat until the butter or margarine has melted. Remove the segments from 2 large or 4 small oranges. Put these into 4 sundae glasses, top with vanilla ice cream and either hot or cold chocolate sauce.

Menu B

Cheese, egg and vegetable pie: cook 1–1¼ lb. carrots; slice half for the pie, put the rest on one side for salad, **Menu C.** Hard-boil 6 eggs, shell and halve 4 eggs; put the rest on one side for the croquettes, **Menu C.**
Make the **white sauce:** heat 2½ oz. butter or margarine in a pan, stir in 2½ oz. flour and cook for several minutes, then gradually blend in 1¼ pints milk. Bring the sauce to the boil and cook until thickened. Pour ¾ pint of the sauce into a basin, add seasoning and 4 oz. grated cheese (leave the remainder of the sauce in the pan for the salad dressing – see recipe under Russian salad, **Menu C**).
To assemble the Cheese, egg and vegetable pie: put the sliced carrots and halved eggs into a pie dish, top with the ¾ pint cheese sauce, then thickly-sliced potatoes and a grating of cheese. Bake for approximately 30 minutes in a moderately hot oven (375–400°F., Gas Mark 5–6) until the potatoes are crisp and golden brown.
Green salad: blend shredded lettuce, cress, and sliced cucumber together and toss in a little oil, vinegar and seasoning.
Malted fruit gâteau [F]: make golden sponge – cream 6 oz. margarine, 6 oz. castor sugar until soft and light. Gradually beat in 3 large eggs, then fold in 6 oz. self-raising flour, 2 oz. Ovaltine and about 2 teaspoons milk to give a soft consistency. Grease and flour 2 6-inch sandwich tins and divide two-thirds of the sponge mixture between these. (Leave the rest in the mixing bowl for the Walnut apple tart, **Menu C**). Bake the sandwich cakes for approximately 18–20 minutes, until firm to the touch, in a moderate oven (350–375°F., Gas Mark 4–5). Turn out and cool, then sandwich together with fruit and cream.

Menu C

Ham croquettes [F]: chop 8 oz. cooked ham, chop 2 hard-boiled eggs. Mix together in a basin with 4 oz. soft breadcrumbs, 1 egg and seasoning (a little chopped spring onion and mixed herbs could be added if wished). Form into 8 finger shapes, coat with beaten egg and roll in crisp breadcrumbs. Either fry in hot fat until crisp and golden brown or put on to a greased baking sheet and bake for 15 minutes towards the top of a hot oven.
Russian salad: first make the *salad dressing* – whisk 1 egg into the ½ pint sauce remaining in the saucepan, with plenty of seasoning and the juice of ½–1 lemon. Cook *GENTLY WITHOUT BOILING* for several minutes. Allow to become cold and use some for the salad and store the rest in a cool place in a screw-topped jar.
To make the salad: dice the potatoes and carrots, chop the beans more finely if necessary, then toss in some of the salad dressing and serve on a bed of crisp lettuce, with halved fresh tomatoes.
Walnut apple tart [F]: line a 7-inch pie plate with short crust pastry, cover with about 12 oz. *thinly* sliced or grated apples, spread with a little apricot jam, then top with the remainder of the golden sponge mixture and about 2 oz. halved walnuts. Bake for approximately 15 minutes in the centre of a hot oven (425–450°F., Gas Mark 6–7) to set the pastry, then lower the heat to moderate (350–375°F., Gas Mark 4–5) for a further 30 minutes until the apples and topping are cooked. Serve cold with cream or ice cream.

The preceding pages give practical examples of meals for 2 days, but here are some other ways in which you can prepare foods to save time: since suggestions are made for home freezing of cooked foods on pages 11 to 12 the following are based on foods that can be cooked and thereafter stored in a refrigerator or cool larder to be used when needed.

Soups:

If you prepare a double quantity you can alter the flavour slightly with additional herbs, vegetables, etc., so that the soup can be served on a second day as a different soup . . . or possibly you could use the soup as a basis for a casserole dish?

Stews:

A stew takes a lot of preparation and most people will agree that it tastes better when re-heated, than on the day it is cooked . . . you could make enough for two days and serve it the second day with a new topping so that it does not taste exactly the same.

Suggested quick toppings for stews:

Put the stew into an ovenproof dish and cover with:

Savoury crumb topping: blend coarse crumbs with melted margarine or butter (allow 1 oz. fat to each 4 oz. coarse crumbs), add plenty of seasoning and a generous amount of chopped parsley. Heat thoroughly in a very moderate oven.

Cheese potato topping: blend 1 oz. margarine and 3 oz. grated cheese to each 1 lb. mashed potatoes. Spread over the stew and top with a little more grated cheese. Heat thoroughly in a moderate oven.

Fluffy crumb topping: beat 2 egg yolks, add seasoning, 2 oz. fine breadcrumbs and 2 oz. grated cheese. Blend in 1 tablespoon milk to give a soft mixture, then add the 2 stiffly beaten egg whites. Heat the stew in an ovenproof dish and when hot spread the fluffy egg mixture on top. Return to a moderate oven for approximately 12-15 minutes until pale golden brown and set.

This topping blends particularly well with a veal stew.

Vegetables:

Cook extra potatoes – sliced they can be fried in fat (sauté potatoes) for another meal. Mashed potatoes can be blended with egg yolk and a little extra butter (Duchesse potatoes) and piled or piped into neat shapes on ovenproof serving dishes and browned in the oven. Other cooked vegetables can be put into salads, as suggested on page 87.

Crumbs, for stuffings, etc.

It takes time to make crumbs for various dishes such as stuffings, or crumb crumble, as page 59: why not prepare extra and store the rest in polythene bags or containers?

The above are just a few suggestions for saving time, but you will discover many others. When you plan your meals, try and think ahead, so that you can save time, washing up, etc.

Making wise use of money

Plan your family meals to take advantage of special 'bargains' in supermarkets or grocers, and to use those foods (fresh vegetables, fruit, etc.) that are in season and therefore at their cheapest and best.

Food is too expensive to waste and the following suggestions give ideas for making use of left-over foods. TAKE CARE, therefore, that the food is **stored correctly** in a cool place, preferably a refrigerator, so that it is in a good condition. If you have a home freezer you can freeze most foods, see page 12, until required.

USING LEFT-OVERS

No matter how carefully one caters, there is bound to be food left. This does not mean it is wasted, for if kept carefully in a cool place – a refrigerator giving the perfect storage – it provides the basis for new and interesting meals. Never 'use up' food if you suspect it has become bad, though, for food poisoning could result.

To use left-over fish

This is probably one of the foods that spoil more easily than any other, so use quickly; serve cold with salad or as:

a) **Fish Cakes** – see recipe for Salmon fish cakes.

b) **Fish Pie [F]** – flake the fish, blend with chopped hard-boiled eggs and anchovy, or a white, cheese or parsley sauce. Put into a pie dish, top with potato and tiny pieces of butter. Put into centre of a moderately hot oven for approximately 30 minutes until heated through, and crisp and brown on top. Garnish with chopped parsley and lemon slices.

To use left-over meat or poultry
a) **Serve cold with salad.**
b) **Use in a quick casserole** – one of the easiest ways to make an appetising casserole if you have no stock or gravy available is to use canned soups, the thicker condensed type of soup is better. ALWAYS HEAT THE MEAT THROUGH THOROUGHLY.

Suggestions for casseroles:
If you have left-over beef: heat a can of vegetable soup, dice the beef and add to the soup, add a little made-mustard to give a more interesting flavour to the soup, or stir in a small quantity of horseradish cream. Canned or frozen vegetables can be added too.
If you have left-over chicken: choose a mushroom or asparagus soup and heat the neatly-diced cooked chicken in this. Add sliced (canned or fresh) green or red pepper or corn, or mixed vegetables.
If you have left-over ham: dice and heat in a cream of chicken soup or a tomato soup, add corn, sliced mushrooms or grated carrot to give more flavour.
If you have left-over duck: heat in a canned consommé, as the thinner stock is better with the rich meat. Thicken with a little cornflour just before serving. Lamb and pork can be heated in consommé as well.

Using left-over vegetables
These can be put into salads, added to a stew towards the end of cooking – not green vegetables, of course – or made into **Bubble and squeak:** mix together equal quantities of mashed potato and cooked, chopped green vegetable. Blend well until quite a smooth texture, adding a little extra seasoning. Heat 1–2 oz. fat in a pan. Put in the mixture, flattening it with a knife. Cook over a slow heat so the bottom of mixture becomes golden brown. Insert a palette or flat bladed knife under the mixture, fold over. Tip on to a hot serving dish.

Bread*
Make into fine crumbs by rubbing through a sieve. Put on to baking trays and crisp in a cool oven. If not sufficiently fine spread on sheets of greaseproof paper, cover with more paper and then with a rolling pin gently and firmly roll. Store in airtight jars and use for coating fish, meat, etc.
Use in a Queen of Puddings.
Make into Melba toast – cut into wafer-thin slices, put on to baking trays and crisp in a very moderate oven.

*To freshen left-over bread, dip quickly into a little water to moisten, then crisp in the oven for about 15 minutes.

Fruit
Add cooked fruit to jellies, being careful to measure the amount of juice so that you do not exceed the pint of liquid. Strain off surplus juice, sieve or beat to a smooth purée and use in a Fruit Fool (see page 67) or Fruit Amber (see page 58).

Using left-over cake
Cut into neat slices, dip in beaten egg then fry in hot butter until golden coloured. Serve for a sweet – as easy fritters – topped with jam. Use plain cake crumbs in Queen of Puddings.

Tips for time saving

● **Grate vegetables,** onion in particular, when you wish them to cook quickly; the cooking time will be much shorter than when the vegetables are finely chopped.

● **Warm citrus fruits,** if you wish to extract the juice quickly (by putting them into hot water for 1–2 minutes). You also have a greater yield of juice. Also, instead of squeezing out the juice from one lemon, why not do several and keep the rest in your refrigerator or even deep freeze in small containers?

● No time to get **crisp breadcrumbs?** – then use crushed cornflakes instead – they give a very good flavour to meats and fish – also crumbled Shredded wheat cakes, see page 75.

● No time to make **breadcrumbs** to use in bread sauce – put a crustless slice of bread into the saucepan, add the milk, bring to the boil and allow to stand for 10 minutes, then beat hard. Add onion, etc., after this.

● No time to make **breadcrumbs** to use in stuffing – put the bread into a basin, pour over boiling water, stand for 5 minutes, then squeeze the bread dry and use in the stuffing.

● Finely **grated orange** or **lemon rinds** keep for some days if stored in covered containers in the refrigerator, or for weeks if put into a deep freeze.

● **Chopped parsley** keeps well for several days if put in a polythene bag or in foil in the refrigerator; it also freezes well.

● Grate any left-over pieces of **cheese** and store in an airtight jar in a cool place. You then always have grated cheese ready to serve as a garnish for soups, for sandwich fillings or to sprinkle over spaghetti and pasta dishes.

● Wipe out **greasy pans** with soft kitchen paper before washing, which then takes only half as long.

● Rinse out a saucepan with cold water BEFORE putting in milk to heat – the saucepan is washed much more quickly.

Menus for main meals

Breakfasts

(*and some variations of savoury dishes to serve at other meals*)

Breakfast is a very important meal, far more important than many people realise; it provides the energy to do a day's work and helps to build up resistance to infection.

When in a hurry there is a tendency to 'skip' breakfast; this is a mistake, for the blood sugar often falls low during the morning – adults and children feel tired – so tend to buy sweets or buns. These can spoil their appetite for lunch and add unwanted weight.

Of course, there are many people who feel they 'cannot cope with breakfast', this may be because they cannot digest or tolerate fat early in the day. In this case they must plan the kind of meal which excludes fat – i.e. cornflakes or porridge, crisp toast or crispbread with marmalade or honey, tea or coffee and fresh fruit. A breakfast that contains a protein dish is much better. If you do not wish to cook eggs, bacon, fish, etc., then serve ready-cooked ham or salami, cheese, or buy some kind of prepared dish (e.g. Scotch eggs) that just needs reheating.

To save time in the mornings: lay the breakfast table overnight, put everything you need in the kitchen to hand, prepare grapefruit and keep it in the refrigerator.

The menus that follow give interesting and easy breakfast menus.

Menus with eggs as main course

Eggs are the quickest cooking and easiest form of protein food for breakfast, and can be cooked in so many different ways.

Wise buying: buy smaller sized eggs for little children so that none is wasted.

Menu:
Grapefruit and orange cocktail
Plain omelette with sliced fresh
 tomatoes
Toast, butter, marmalade
Tea or coffee

Grapefruit and orange cocktail [F]

Cut away the peel from 1 large grapefruit and 2 large oranges in such a way as to cut away the pith as well. Cut the fruit into segments, removing pips, and put into grapefruit glasses. Sweeten to taste. This is often popular with children who sometimes find grapefruit a little 'biting', and it does encourage young ones to eat them.

To Vary:
Hasty cocktail: use canned grapefruit and mandarin orange segments.
Pineapple grapefruit cocktail: blend fresh or canned pineapple and grapefruit.

Plain omelette

cooking time: few minutes

you will need for 4 servings:

4–6 eggs	1 oz. butter
seasoning	
little water (see method)	**to serve:**
	4 tomatoes

1 Beat the eggs and seasoning and add about 1–1½ tablespoons water, if wished, to give a lighter omelette.
2 Heat the butter in the pan* and when hot pour in the eggs.

3 Allow the mixture to set in a thin film on the bottom of the pan.
4 It is time then to 'work' the omelette, this means loosening the edge of the mixture from the sides of the pan, tilting the pan, so the liquid egg flows to the sides and then to the bottom of the pan, so ensuring the omelette cooks quickly and is light – a slowly cooked omelette is tough, unappetising and rather heavy.
5 Slip a palette knife or small fish slice under the omelette and fold away from the handle, then tip on to a hot dish and garnish with the sliced tomatoes.

By serving the tomatoes cold you save cooking time, but when fresh tomatoes are an indifferent quality then cook them and serve with the omelette.

*For a perfect omelette use a medium sized pan for this amount of eggs; too small a pan means too great a depth of mixture and a too slowly cooked omelette. Too large a pan means a very thin layer of egg which becomes dry in cooking.

To vary:
Although perhaps not suitable for breakfast, omelettes may be filled with cooked vegetables or heated canned kidneys. There are also other suggestions for omelettes on page 44.

Shopping reminders:

grapefruit, oranges, eggs, tomatoes (*also needed:* seasoning, butter, bread, marmalade or honey, tea, coffee, milk and sugar. These you will, of course, buy regularly).

Menu:
Mixed fruit cocktail
Boiled eggs
Toast, butter and jam or marmalade
Tea or coffee

Mixed fruit cocktail

Mix together equal quantities of fresh or canned orange, grapefruit and pineapple juices. Flavour with a few fresh mint leaves, if wished.

Boiled eggs

You can either lower the eggs carefully into cold water or put into the water when it is boiling.

If putting into cold water – allow 3 minutes cooking from the time the water comes to the boil, if you like a really soft-boiled egg (very new-laid or slightly firmer eggs take 4 minutes). Allow approximately 9–10 minutes for a hard-boiled egg.

If putting into boiling water – allow $3\frac{1}{2}$–4 minutes for a really soft-boiled egg, allow longer for a very new-laid or slightly firmer egg.

Hard-boiled eggs take 10 minutes.

To vary: (many of these are more suitable for a main dish)

Eggs au gratin: soft-boil or hard-boil the eggs, shell, put into an ovenproof dish, top with cheese sauce, see page 78, grated cheese and crumbs, and brown under a hot grill.

Tomato eggs: soft-boil or hard-boil the eggs, shell, put into a serving dish, top with skinned tomatoes, cooked to make a purée and seasoned well (or with tomato sauce) and serve with grated cheese.

Stuffed eggs: hard-boil the eggs, shell and halve, remove the yolks, blend with a little butter or mayonnaise and a choice of flavourings – curry powder or mashed sardines or finely chopped ham or liver pâté or grated cheese. Pile back into the halved white cases. For breakfast they can be served on slices of fresh brown or white bread and butter; for a cocktail savoury they can be cut into quarters; for a main meal, serve on a bed of salad.

Shopping reminders:

canned, frozen or fresh orange juice, fresh grapefruit or canned or frozen grapefruit juice, canned pineapple juice, mint (optional), eggs (*also needed:* seasoning to serve with the boiled eggs, bread, butter, jam or marmalade, tea, coffee, milk, sugar).

Menu:
Stewed prunes
Scrambled eggs on toast
Tea or coffee

Stewed prunes

Cover 8 oz. dried prunes with cold water or strained weak tea (this sounds unusual, but is very good). Put to soak either overnight or in the morning of the day before serving this menu (or soak a double amount and use the extra prunes for serving with bacon, see page 24 or for a quick snack, see page 89). After some hours soaking, simmer gently for about 1 hour until tender, add sugar to taste and a little lemon juice if wished.

Remember, though, you can buy ready tenderised prunes, which obviates the necessity of soaking, or you can serve canned prunes instead.

To vary:
Stewed figs: as above – weak coffee instead of water gives an excellent flavour.

Scrambled eggs

Allow 1 or 2 eggs per person. Beat lightly with a little seasoning. If you wish a less rich scrambled egg, allow $\frac{1}{2}$–1 tablespoon milk or top of the milk per egg. For about 4–6 eggs, heat 1 oz. butter or margarine in a saucepan and when melted add the eggs, cook *gently*, stirring with a wooden spoon until lightly set. Pile on to hot buttered toast. It is a mistake to keep scrambled eggs waiting, so toast the bread, spread with butter and keep hot while cooking the eggs.

Note: the saucepan used for scrambling eggs is easier to wash up if this is filled with cold water *immediately the eggs are dished up*, and left soaking during breakfast; or use a silicone (non-stick) pan.

To vary: (suitable for light meals as well as breakfast)
Anchovy eggs: add a few drops anchovy essence to the beaten eggs, or if serving for a quick supper dish, top the scrambled eggs with canned anchovy fillets (this dish is generally called Scotch Woodcock).

Bean scramble: heat the contents of a small can of baked beans in the butter, then add 4–6 beaten eggs, season lightly and scramble. Children love this – it also is a good way of 'ekeing out' eggs to serve a greater number of people.

Carrot scramble: toss 1–2 grated raw carrots in the hot butter, then add the eggs and scramble in the usual way. Children sometimes dislike the soft texture of a scrambled egg and this gives a crispness they enjoy.

Cheese scramble: add 1–2 oz. grated cheese (Cheddar or Gruyère) to 4–6 beaten eggs – take particular care not to overcook this variation, otherwise the cheese becomes tough.

Chicken eggs: add finely diced cooked chicken to the eggs before cooking, or heat chicken in butter first if the pieces are fairly solid.

Ham eggs: add finely chopped ham to the eggs before cooking; salami or other cooked meats may be used instead if wished.

Salmon eggs: heat a tiny can of flaked salmon in the butter, then add the eggs and cook. Other fish (tuna especially) could be used.

Vegetable scramble: heat cooked or well-drained canned mixed vegetables in the butter, and then add the eggs and scramble.

Shopping reminders:

prunes, sugar, lemon (optional), eggs (*also needed:* seasoning, bread, butter, tea – for prunes if using this flavouring – coffee, milk).

Menu:
Poached eggs on toast
Bread and butter
Fresh fruit
Tea or coffee

Poached eggs

The eggs may either be cooked in a 'proper' egg poacher or in a pan of boiling water – the latter gives a softer type of poached egg.

If using a poacher: put a small piece (about ¼ oz.) butter or margarine into each metal cup and melt this over the boiling water in the base of the pan. Break each egg into a cup and then pour carefully into the metal container and put on the lid. Poach until set, approximately 3 minutes, then slide on to hot buttered toast.

If using hot water method: heat the water in a saucepan or frying pan, add a good pinch salt

and a few drops vinegar if wished (this helps to keep the egg-white from spreading out). Slip the eggs from the cup one by one into the gently boiling water. As the egg goes into the water, move the water with a spoon so that you 'gather' the egg-white together. Cook for 2–3 minutes until set. Lift out with a fish slice and allow to drain over the pan for a minute, then put on to hot buttered toast.

Note: you can also put an old greased pastry cutter into the water, pour the egg in this, leave for about 1 minute to set the outer white, then lift up the pastry cutter and use again for the next egg. Or put several cutters into the water at the same time, if the pan is large enough. If using this method, omit the vinegar.

To vary: (some of these variations are more suitable for a light main dish)

Poached eggs au gratin: put the eggs on to hot toast or a bed of creamed potatoes, top with a little cream from the top of the milk and a thick layer of grated cheese, or thinly sliced cheese and crisp breadcrumbs (raspings), brown under a hot grill.

Poached eggs Florentine: put on a bed of cooked spinach, frozen or canned, top with cheese sauce, see page 78, sprinkle with a little grated cheese and brown in the oven, or under the grill.

Spanish poached eggs: for 4 people you need to chop 12 oz. skinned tomatoes, 1 medium onion, 1 green pepper. Put all of these into a frying pan in 2 oz. hot butter or margarine, season very well. Simmer until a soft purée; if becoming rather thick dilute with a little water. Break the eggs carefully into this mixture and poach. Serve with crusty bread and butter.

Shopping reminders:

eggs, fresh fruit (*also needed:* bread, seasoning, butter, tea, coffee, milk, sugar).

Menu:
Hot grapefruit
Baked eggs
Hot rolls with butter and marmalade
Tea or coffee

Hot grapefruit

Halve the grapefruit, loosen the segments and remove any pips. Spread with a very little butter, sprinkle with sugar (brown if possible) to taste, or with sugar and honey or just honey or golden syrup. Add a dusting of powdered cinnamon or spice if wished. Either heat for a few minutes under the grill, or, since you are using the oven, put into the oven (in the hottest part) for about 10 minutes.

To vary: top grapefruit with a little sherry before heating.

Baked eggs

Grease small individual ovenproof dishes, or one larger dish, with a generous amount of butter or margarine. Break the eggs carefully into the dishes or dish. Top with seasoning, a little cream from the top of the milk and a very small amount of butter. Bake for approximately 10 minutes just above the centre of a moderately hot oven (375–400°F., Gas Mark 5–6). Serve with a teaspoon.

To vary: (possibly most of the variations are more suitable for high tea or supper)

Eggs with asparagus: put chopped canned asparagus tips in the dishes and break an egg on top.

Cheese eggs: put a layer of grated or sliced cheese on the bottom of the dish, add the eggs, then the cream, seasoning and a layer of grated cheese.

Ham eggs: put finely chopped ham at the base of the dish (other cooked meats could be used).

Swiss omelette or oven-baked omelette: as cheese eggs, but beat the eggs with seasoning before adding to the dish.

Shopping reminders:

grapefruit, brown sugar, powdered cinnamon, rolls, eggs (*also needed:* seasoning, butter or margarine, marmalade, tea, coffee, milk, sugar).

Menus with meat as main course

Cold meat, particularly cooked ham or tongue or sliced corned beef, is a quick protein food for breakfast, so use it to make a change from bacon or sausages.

Wise buying: good streaky bacon is an economical 'buy' if you do not mind a certain amount of fat. If you prefer leaner bacon for breakfast then buy back bacon. Make sure the bacon looks moist and not dry and hard. Try the more economical beef sausages for a change.

Menu:
Tomato juice
Sausage and bacon cakes
**   with fried mushrooms**
Hot rolls, butter and honey
Tea or coffee

Sausage and bacon cakes [F] with fried mushrooms

cooking time: 15 minutes

you will need for 4–6 servings:

1 lb. pork *or* beef sausagemeat	
2 rashers streaky bacon	**to fry:** little fat
pinch mixed herbs (optional)	
approximately ½ oz. flour	**to serve:** 2–4 oz. mushrooms

1 Put the sausagemeat into a basin and add the bacon (cut into very thin strips with kitchen scissors) and the herbs.

2 If you like crisp bacon this could be fried until golden brown before adding to the sausage-meat.

3 Form the mixture into round flat cakes, coat in the flour and fry in a very little fat until brown, then lower heat and cook steadily for another 5 minutes. Place on to a hot dish and fry the mushrooms in the remaining fat.

Note: Good quality mushrooms need *not* be skinned. Wash them well, and trim the base of the stems. The sausage cakes can be prepared overnight and left in the refrigerator.

To vary: [F]
Sausage tomato cakes: add 2 skinned chopped tomatoes to the sausagemeat; if the mixture seems a little soft, chill in the refrig-

erator before forming into cakes. Omit the bacon if wished.

Sausage herb cakes: blend a generous tablespoon freshly chopped mixed herbs, or all chopped parsley, with the sausagemeat. Do not use dried herbs instead in this quantity. Omit the bacon if wished.

Sausage oatmeal cakes: coat the cakes with well-seasoned oatmeal or rolled oats before frying.

Sausage potato cakes: use half sausage-meat and half mashed potatoes and season well.

Shopping reminders:

tomato juice (canned or bottled), sausagemeat, bacon, herbs, flour, fat, mushrooms, rolls (*also needed:* butter, honey, tea, coffee, milk, sugar).

Menu:
Bacon and prunes
Cinnamon toast
Tea or coffee

Bacon and prunes

Cut the rinds from the bacon and fry or grill in the usual way, then heat the prunes, either in a little prune juice or in the bacon fat (if using a frying pan).

Note: fry the rinds *with* the rashers of bacon to give extra fat. If allowed to become very crisp these bacon rinds are an excellent cocktail snack, and when broken into tiny pieces take the place of potato crisps to serve with a drink.

To vary:

Bacon and apple rings: core cooking apples, but do not peel. Cut into $\frac{1}{4}$–$\frac{1}{2}$ inch rings and cook steadily in the bacon fat with the bacon. Sprinkle with a little sugar if wished, just before serving.

Bacon and cheese slices (more suitable for high tea or supper): when the bacon is nearly cooked put fairly thick slices of Cheddar, Gruyère, Dutch or processed cheese into the pan and cook for a few minutes only, until just melted.

Bacon and eggs: fry the bacon first, then lift on to a hot dish (unless cooking a very small amount, then push the rashers of bacon to one side of the pan). Break the eggs on to a saucer, or in a cup, and slip the eggs into the hot fat (if the bacon has not given sufficient fat then add a little extra before cooking the eggs). Cook until just set. If you wish to give a white skin over the yolk, 'baste' (i.e. spoon) the fat over the egg-yolk as it cooks. If you like a crisp bottom to the egg, make sure the fat is *very* hot when the eggs go into the pan.

Bacon and mushrooms: fry the bacon first then add the prepared mushrooms, see page 23 and fry, or cook the bacon on the grid of the grill pan with the mushrooms in the pan below.

Bacon and tomatoes: cook as bacon and mushrooms; season the halved tomatoes well and add a pinch of sugar too.

Bacon and sausages: since the sausages take longer to cook than bacon, put these under the hot grill or in the pan first. Modern sausage skins do not 'burst' as easily as in the past, so many manufacturers no longer advocate pricking the skins. *Grill* steadily, turning round from time to time, until golden brown, then add the bacon. If *frying*, grease the pan very lightly so that the sausages will not stick to the pan. Fry steadily, turning round several times, then add the bacon. Frozen sausages may be cooked from the frozen state.

Cinnamon toast

Toast the bread, spread with butter or margarine, and sprinkle with powdered cinnamon.

Shopping reminders:

bacon, prunes, powdered cinnamon (*also needed:* bread, butter or margarine, tea, coffee, milk, sugar).

Menus with fish as main course

Although not usual, fried or grilled white fish is an excellent breakfast dish: so are fish fingers; fish cakes; as well as smoked fish. As you will be buying the fish the day before it is required, store it carefully. Remember there is very good frozen fish available which may be more convenient to keep overnight.

Menu:
Apple and orange compote
Poached haddock
Toast, butter and marmalade
Tea or coffee

Apple and orange compote [F]

cooking time: 10–15 minutes

you will need for 8 servings:

3–4 large oranges   2 lb. cooking apples
water
sugar to taste

1 Grate the rind from the oranges – do this finely, so you use only the top orange 'zest' and none of the bitter white pith.
2 Squeeze out the orange juice and add enough water to give $\frac{1}{2}$–$\frac{3}{4}$ pint liquid (depending upon amount of juice you like).
3 Put the orange rind and juice into a large saucepan, or you can even use a deep frying pan. The reason for a large diameter pan is that the apples should be covered in the liquid as they cook.
4 Add sugar to taste, and the peeled apples cut into neat segments.
5 Simmer steadily, turning the apples so that they become coated with the orange liquid; serve cold.

Note: These are also delicious for a dessert.

To vary: [F]
Another version of this dish is to cook the apples in water, sugar and the finely grated orange rind, then to add the segments of fresh orange when the apples are cooked and cold. This retains the Vitamin C in the fruit.

Instead of fresh fruit use canned mandarin oranges, adding the liquid from the can to the water and sugar, or use canned pineapple, apricots or prunes.

Poached haddock

You can buy frozen haddock 'in a bag' and you 'boil in the bag', as directed, so saving the smell of cooking, but if using freshly smoked haddock (or cod) then allow about 4–6 oz. per person. Cut the fillets or the whole fish into portions, removing fins and tail. Put into cold water, bring water to the boil, lower the heat and simmer for approximately 5–6 minutes, depending upon thickness of the fish. Drain and serve topped with butter or margarine.

To vary:
Cook gently in milk and water. Top with poached eggs.

Shopping reminders:
oranges, cooking apples, sugar, haddock (*also needed:* bread, butter, marmalade, tea, coffee, milk).

Menu:
Orange juice
Grilled herrings
Crispbread, butter, honey
Tea or coffee

Grilled herrings

Ask the fishmonger to bone the herrings for you as they take a shorter cooking time when filleted. If this has not been done, cut off the head, then split the fish under the stomach, until it is opened out flat, lay the cut side downwards on the table or chopping board. Run your thumb or finger down the skin of the fish over the backbone (do this quite firmly). Turn the fish over, and you will find the backbone, with all the little bones, can be removed very easily. Cut the whole fish into two fillets. Season the herring and brush with a little fat and grill steadily. The fillets do not need turning but, if you fold the boned fish over, this is thick, so must be grilled on either side. Serve with slices of lemon.

To vary:
Fried herrings: coat the herring with seasoned flour or oatmeal or rolled oats and fry in a little hot fat until tender.
Baked herrings [F]: wrap the fish in buttered foil and bake for approximately 20–25 minutes in the centre of a hot oven (400–425°F., Gas

Mark 6–7). The boned herrings are delicious if stuffed with sliced uncooked tomatoes and mushrooms – seasoned well. The cooking time should then be extended to 30–35 minutes.

Shopping reminders:
oranges or canned or frozen orange juice, herrings, lemon, crispbread (*also needed:* seasoning, butter, honey, tea, coffee, milk, sugar).

Menu:
Cornflakes and bananas
'Jugged' kippers
Toast, butter, marmalade
Tea or coffee

'Jugged' kippers

When in a hurry it is advisable to buy kipper fillets, which are ready-boned. If frozen they need not be allowed to defrost before cooking. Put the kipper fillets or kippers into a tall jug or container. Pour over rapidly boiling water, cover the container and leave for about 5 minutes (a little longer for frozen kippers). Lift out, drain and serve.

This method of cooking has the merit that you can leave the kippers unattended. If you like them crisp, however, either grill as herring or proceed as above, drain, then top with a little butter and grill for 2 minutes only, or fry for a few minutes.

Note: Remember to cover the grill pan with foil, so that it is easy to clean.

Bloaters can be grilled or fried, as a change from kippers.

Shopping reminders:
cornflakes, bananas, milk, sugar, kippers (*also needed:* bread, butter, marmalade, tea, coffee).

Your automatic oven for breakfast

It is a practical idea to make use of your automatic oven for preparing breakfast dishes. The meal is put in the oven at night and the controls set so that breakfast is ready at the time you want it.

Bacon: remove rinds, arrange on an oven-proof plate as you would in the frying pan, i.e. so that the fat of one rasher is under the lean of the next rasher. In this way you keep the lean part moist. Cover with foil so the bacon does not harden, unless you like very crisp bacon. (Thin rashers would need about 20 minutes in the very hottest part of a moderate oven, or can stay for about 30–35 minutes if you put in a cooler part of the oven, to serve with sausages.)

Eggs: put into greased containers, cover with foil (so that the eggs do not dry). These take about 20 minutes in the coolest part of a moderate oven.

Fish: if very thin fillets, treat as bacon: if thick fish, then as sausages.

Porridge: measure the rolled oats as instructed on the packet. To have ready for an automatic oven it is advisable to pour boiling water over the rolled oats, to stir well, cover the ovenproof dish and put in the coolest part of a moderate oven. Stir well before serving.

Sausages: these need not be covered, just put into ovenproof dish or tin and bake for about 30–35 minutes in the hottest part of a moderate oven.

To heat rolls: wrap in foil and put at the very bottom of a gas oven or the coolest part of an electric oven or in the warming compartment.

Remember to put plates in the warming drawer, if you have one.

Meals that take less than 15 minutes cooking

In this section are meals that require no cooking, i.e. the ingredients are bought ready-cooked or you use foods that can be heated or cooked within a very short time. It is possible to have very satisfying meals that are prepared quickly. The dishes are in the order of serving the menu, since everything is so quick and simple. (In the more complicated menus, starting on page 31, the dishes of each menu are arranged in the order in which they should be prepared.)

Shopping reminders:
there are quite a few variations to a number of dishes – but the shopping reminders refer to the basic menu only.

Menu:
Corned beef and potato mould
Jelly whip
Cheese and biscuits

Corned beef and potato mould

no cooking

you will need for 4–6 servings:

medium can new potatoes	12 oz. cooked corned beef
1 tablespoon chopped parsley	mayonnaise to bind
2–3 tablespoons peeled diced cucumber	
2 oz. small mushrooms	**to garnish:** lettuce, cucumber, tomatoes

1 Open the can of potatoes, drain well and cut into neat pieces, add the other ingredients, slicing the mushrooms and dicing the beef.
2 Gradually stir in enough mayonnaise to bind.
3 Put into a plain mould or basin and leave for about 30 minutes, then turn out on to a bed of lettuce and garnish with the salad ingredients.

Note: sliced uncooked mushrooms are excellent in salads.

To vary:
Ham and potato mould: use diced ham in place of corned beef – a diced dessert apple and a chopped green pepper may be added if wished. In this case omit the mushrooms.
Fish and potato mould: cut cooked fish into neat pieces or flake coarsely, depending upon the type of fish. Blend with the ingredients in the basic salad. If using cooked or rollmop herrings, include a diced dessert apple.
Cheese and potato mould: use diced Cheddar or processed cheese in place of corned beef.

Jelly whip

Make a fruit flavoured jelly with only $\frac{1}{2}$ pint very hot water. When cold and just beginning to stiffen (this will happen fairly quickly, because of the small amount of water) add a large block of ice cream and whisk hard into the jelly. Pile into a serving dish.

To vary:
Jelly cream: make the jelly with just under $\frac{3}{4}$ pint water. When beginning to stiffen, whisk in $\frac{1}{4}$ pint thin cream or evaporated milk.
Yoghourt jelly: make the jelly with just under $\frac{3}{4}$ pint water. When cold stir in a carton (approximately $\frac{1}{4}$ pint) yoghourt – the fruit flavoured is a good idea. Put into the dish or mould and allow to set.

Shopping reminders:
Corned beef mould: canned potatoes, parsley, cucumber, mushrooms, corned beef, mayonnaise, lettuce, tomatoes.
Dessert: jelly, ice cream.
Cheese and biscuits, butter.

Menu:
Grapefruit
Cheeseburgers with salad
Ice cream with ginger apricot sauce

Cheeseburgers with salad

cooking time: 10–15 minutes

you will need for 4 servings:

1 oz. fat	**for the salad:**
large packet frozen	lettuce
hamburgers *or*	tomatoes
similar meat cakes	cucumber
4 slices Cheddar *or*	canned sweetcorn
processed cheese*	(optional)

*This adds extra protein

1 Spread half the fat on top of the hamburgers.
2 Put under a hot grill and cook as directed on the packet, turning half-way and spreading with the remainder of the fat.
3 When cooked, top each meat cake with a piece of cheese and brown under the grill until the cheese has melted.
4 Serve with the salad.

Ice cream and apricot ginger sauce

cooking time: few minutes

you will need for 4 servings:

for the sauce:	1–2 oz. preserved
1 lemon	ginger
4 tablespoons	
apricot jam	1 large block ice
	cream

1 Grate the 'zest' from the lemon, and put with its juice and the jam into a saucepan, or in a basin if you do not wish to heat the sauce.
2 Heat for a few minutes, or blend well.
3 Add the chopped preserved ginger.
4 Put the ice cream into sundae glasses and top with the hot or cold sauce.

To vary:
There are many sauces you can make which blend well with ice cream – here are some easy suggestions (all are enough for 4 portions).

Almond and orange sauce
Blend the grated rind and juice of 1 orange with about 3–4 tablespoons jelly marmalade. Heat until melted then add 1 oz. chopped blanched almonds.

Butterscotch sauce
Heat 2 oz. butter with 4 oz. brown sugar until the sugar has melted. Stir in 2–3 tablespoons milk or thin cream, and heat together for 1–2 minutes only. Serve cold.

Caramel sauce
Stir 3 oz. granulated or castor sugar and 3 tablespoons water over a low heat until the sugar has melted. Boil steadily until a golden coloured caramel, then add a further 2–3 tablespoons water and blend in with the caramel. Allow to cool.
Note: It is worthwhile making a larger quantity of this and storing to use as required.

Date and syrup sauce
Heat 4–5 tablespoons golden syrup in a saucepan until slightly darkened in colour (this makes an easy caramel if you boil until golden brown), then add about 2 oz. chopped dates.

Fruit sauce
Take about $\frac{1}{4}$ pint syrup from a can of fruit, blend with 1 teaspoon arrowroot or cornflour and 1–2 tablespoons sieved apricot jam or redcurrant jelly. Stir over a low heat until the jelly has dissolved and the sauce is clear. Add about 4–5 tablespoons chopped canned fruit and pour over the ice cream – serve hot or cold.

Shopping reminders:
Grapefruit and sugar.
Cheeseburgers: fat, frozen hamburgers, cheese, lettuce, tomatoes, cucumber, canned sweetcorn (or other salad ingredients).
Dessert: lemon, apricot jam, preserved ginger, ice cream.

Menu:
Fresh orange juice
Tuna salad with crispbread and butter
Ginger snaps

Tuna salad with crispbread and butter

Put 3 eggs on to boil until firm. Open a medium sized can of tuna fish; flake the fish and blend with mayonnaise, 1 chopped green pepper, 2–3 tablespoons chopped celery or sliced, stuffed olives. Arrange on a bed of lettuce and garnish with halved tomatoes, sliced cucumbers and the halved hard-boiled eggs. (If still warm the eggs are very pleasant in the salad.) Serve with crispbread and butter.

To vary:
Use ready cooked diced tongue in place of tuna fish – omit green pepper and add small cocktail onions and chopped pickled walnuts instead.
Use flaked salmon in place of tuna fish. Omit green pepper and use chopped asparagus instead.

Ginger snaps

Buy ready-made brandy snaps.
To fill: whip ¼ pint thick cream and blend in 1 oz. chopped glacé cherries, 1 oz. chopped crystallised ginger. Put the cream mixture into the brandy snaps.

Shopping reminders:

Fresh orange juice.
Tuna salad: eggs, can tuna, mayonnaise, green pepper, celery or stuffed olives, lettuce, tomatoes, cucumber.
Ginger snaps: brandy snaps, thick cream, glacé cherries, crystallised ginger.

Menu:
Piperade with fingers of toast
Stuffed ham rolls, asparagus
Fresh fruit

Piperade with fingers of toast

cooking time: few minutes

you will need for 4 servings:

1 small onion	4 eggs
2 tomatoes	seasoning
1 green pepper	**to garnish:**
2 oz. butter	slices of toast

1 Peel and grate the onion, skin and chop the tomatoes, and chop the pepper, discarding seeds and core.
2 Heat the butter in a saucepan and fry the vegetables for about 5–6 minutes until just soft, do not let these become over soft, it is pleasant to keep a little of the texture of the pepper).
3 Beat the eggs, season, pour into the pan, then scramble lightly. Pile on to 4 hot plates and garnish with toast. Serve at once.

Stuffed ham rolls

Fill rolled thin slices of ham with soft cream cheese (you need about 6 oz. cooked ham and 2–3 oz. cream cheese or cheese spread). Arrange on a dish and garnish with lettuce and top with canned well-drained asparagus tips.

To vary:
Blend 1–2 teaspoons of chopped gherkins, capers or parsley with the cheese.
Blend a little curry powder and chopped chutney with the cheese, or use finely chopped mustard pickle.
Omit the cream cheese and fill with a tomato breadcrumb mixture, made by blending 2 oz. soft breadcrumbs, 2 skinned chopped tomatoes, 2–3 chopped gherkins and seasoning – this not only makes the ham more interesting, it keeps it very moist.

Shopping reminders:

Piperade: onion, tomatoes, green pepper, butter, salt, pepper, eggs, bread.
Stuffed ham rolls: cooked ham, cream cheese, lettuce, canned asparagus tips.
Dessert: fresh fruit.

Menu:
Parmesan fish cakes
**   with tomato and pepper salad**
Lemon stuffed peaches

Parmesan fish cakes with tomato and pepper salad

Fry frozen fish cakes on either side until nearly brown, then lift from the pan and drain on absorbent paper, roll in grated Parmesan cheese and replace in the pan for 1 minute.

To make the salad, slice tomatoes thinly and cut a deseeded green pepper into thin slices, mix together and toss in a little well-seasoned oil and vinegar.

Lemon stuffed peaches

Allow 2 canned peach halves per person. Put 8 peach halves on a serving dish. Blend 2 crushed macaroon biscuits (medium size) with the grated rind of 1 lemon, 1 tablespoon lemon juice and 1 good tablespoon lemon curd. Pile the crumb mixture into the peaches. Serve with cream.

To vary:
To make a more substantial sweet, arrange each peach half on a slice of Swiss roll, moistened with the peach syrup blended with a little fresh lemon juice – you could then allow just one peach half per person.

Shopping reminders:
Parmesan fish cakes: fat, frozen fish cakes, Parmesan cheese, tomatoes, green pepper, salt, pepper, oil, vinegar.
Dessert: canned peaches, macaroon biscuits, lemon, lemon curd, cream.

Menu:
Savoury macaroni with peas
Apricot tipsy cake

Savoury macaroni with peas

cooking time: 15 minutes

you will need for 4 servings:

4 oz. quick-cooking elbow length macaroni	shake of garlic salt
seasoning	**to garnish:**
medium size can tomatoes	large packet frozen peas
4 oz. shelled prawns or shrimps	

1 Put the macaroni into 2 pints boiling salted water. Cook for 7 minutes from the time the liquid comes to the boil; strain.

2 Meanwhile heat the tomatoes with the prawns and seasoning; cook the peas.

3 Tip the strained macaroni into the tomato mixture, toss together and serve on a hot dish with a border of cooked peas.

To vary:
Use another pasta instead of macaroni.
Macaroni marinara: add chopped anchovy fillets and chopped fried bacon to the tomato mixture; omit prawns. Top with grated cheese.
Macaroni vegetable medley: tip a large packet of mixed frozen vegetables into the tomatoes. Cook until the vegetables are tender. Omit the peas and prawns and serve with plenty of grated cheese.
Macaroni and fish Milanaise: add diced cooked white fish to the tomato mixture instead of prawns *or* dilute the tomato mixture with approximately $\frac{1}{2}$ can of water. Cut the un-cooked fish into neat pieces and poach in the tomato mixture until tender.
Macaroni and ham Milanaise: add diced cooked ham to the tomato mixture; omit the prawns.

Apricot tipsy cake [F]

Open a medium sized can of apricots. Blend about $\frac{1}{4}$ pint of the syrup from the can with 2 tablespoons sherry. Split a plain bought sponge cake, soak the bottom half with about 4 table-spoons of the liquid, and sandwich with chopped apricots. Top with the second half of the sponge, moisten this with the remaining liquid and top with the rest of the apricots. Serve with cream or ice cream.

To vary:
Use other fruit instead of apricots.

Shopping reminders:
Savoury macaroni: quick-cooking macaroni, salt, pepper, canned tomatoes, prawns, garlic salt, peas.
Dessert: sponge cake, canned apricots, sherry, cream or ice cream.

Meals that need up to 30 minutes cooking

In this section are menus that can be cooked within 30 minutes, and require the minimum of preparation. Sometimes it is necessary to start to cook the dessert *before* the main dish or the main dish *before* the first course, so you will find the menu given in the correct order of serving, but the actual dishes arranged in the order you will start to cook them. Many of the menus have three courses, naturally one of these may be omitted if wished.

Menu:
Onion soup
Egg and vegetable cream
Fresh fruit

Egg and vegetable cream

cooking time: 25 minutes

you will need for 4 servings:

for the sauce:
1 oz. butter *or* margarine
1 oz. flour
½ pint milk
seasoning

to garnish:
2 tomatoes

4–6 eggs
large packet mixed frozen vegetables *or* canned vegetables
3 tablespoons thin cream

1 Make the white sauce as page 77.
2 Hard-boil the eggs for 10 minutes and crack, plunge into cold water for a few minutes and shell.
3 Tip the frozen vegetables into the sauce and simmer gently, stirring well until tender, if the sauce is getting too thick add a little more water or milk.
If using canned vegetables, drain, add to the sauce and heat.
4 When the vegetables are tender (or hot) then stir in the cream, add more seasoning if wished, reheat gently.
5 Put into a hot dish, top with the halved eggs and the sliced tomatoes.

To vary:
Cheese and vegetable cream: add 6 oz. grated cheese to the vegetable mixture and the

cream. Heat until cheese has melted – do not over-cook. Or use a little less cheese, if wished, and add the hard-boiled eggs, and sliced tomatoes.

Ham, egg and vegetable cream: make the sauce, cook the vegetables as the recipe above, then add 4–6 oz. diced lean cooked ham, the cream, and top with the halved hard-boiled eggs. Garnish with the sliced tomatoes.

Onion soup

cooking time: 15–20 minutes

you will need for 4 servings:

2 oz. butter *or* margarine
3 large onions

to garnish:
1–2 oz. grated cheese

1½ pints canned consommé *or* water and 3 beef stock cubes
seasoning

1 Heat the butter or margarine in a saucepan.
2 Peel and grate the onions coarsely (this shortens cooking time a great deal).
3 Toss the onions in the butter for about 10 minutes, stirring from time to time to make sure they do not become over-brown.
4 Add the liquid and bring to the boil, lower the heat, season as required.
5 Simmer for 5–10 minutes until the onions are very soft.
6 Serve in hot soup bowls, topped with cheese.

To vary:
French onion soup: proceed as above, if time permits slice the onions very thinly and cook for a longer period. Top the soup with slices of French bread or toast, sprinkle with the grated cheese (use Gruyère or Parmesan if possible) and put the soup bowls or tureen under the grill to brown the cheese.

Onion and tomato soup: use tomato juice in place of consommé.

Shopping reminders:
Soup: butter or margarine, onions, canned consommé or stock cubes, seasoning, cheese.

Egg and vegetable cream: butter or margarine, flour, milk, eggs, frozen or canned vegetables, thin cream, seasoning, tomatoes.
Dessert: fresh fruit.

Menu:
Prawn chowder
Kidneys and hard-boiled eggs with toast or creamed potatoes
Buttered cabbage
Orange condé

Orange condé

cooking time: few minutes

you will need for 4 servings:

	to glaze:
1 can creamed rice	2–3 tablespoons jelly marmalade
4 dessert oranges	2 tablespoons water

1 Put the rice into a basin.
2 Cut away the peel from the oranges so that you cut away the white pith as well, then cut the fruit into neat slices, discarding any pips.
3 Mix half the fruit with the rice and put into 4 dishes, top with the remainder of the orange segments.
4 Melt the marmalade with the water; when it has cooled for a few minutes, brush or spread over the fruit.

To vary:
Use other fresh or canned fruit, and use red-currant jelly or strained jam for the glaze.

Kidneys and hard-boiled eggs with toast or creamed potatoes

cooking time: 10–12 minutes

you will need for 4 servings:

	to serve:
4–6 eggs	4 slices buttered toast *or* creamed potatoes
medium sized can of kidneys	
2–3 tablespoons water *or* water and port wine	to garnish:
	chopped parsley

1 Cook the eggs until hard-boiled, crack and shell.

2 Meanwhile, heat the kidneys with the water, or water and wine.
3 Halve the eggs and put on the buttered toast or a bed of creamed potatoes, top with the very hot kidneys and with the chopped parsley. Serve at once, either with a mixed salad or with a green vegetable.
Use dehydrated potatoes for speed.

Buttered cabbage

Fresh cabbage can be cooked very quickly if shredded finely. Put enough water into the saucepan to give a depth of 1 inch, add salt and bring to the boil. Shred the cabbage finely and *gradually* put into the boiling water; if all the cabbage is added at one time the water stops boiling. Cover the pan and cook for about 5–6 minutes until the cabbage is tender, but still 'nutty'.
Strain and toss in a little butter.

To vary:
Spiced cabbage: fry a little grated onion in the butter, when tender add the strained cabbage and a good grating of nutmeg.
Apple and cabbage: toss 1 or 2 grated peeled dessert apples in the butter, add the strained cabbage and reheat for a few minutes.

Prawn chowder

cooking time: few minutes

you will need for 4 servings:

2 oz. frozen prawns	small piece cucumber
large can tomato soup	

1 If using frozen prawns they should be allowed to defrost – the safest method is to put these in the cabinet of the refrigerator during the day.
2 Heat the soup, add the chopped prawns and the peeled diced cucumber and heat again for several minutes.

To vary:
Chicken and corn chowder: add canned sweetcorn and diced cooked ham to a cream of chicken soup.
Mixed vegetable chowder: add cooked or canned vegetables to tomato, chicken or asparagus soups.

Note: A chowder should be a thick consistency with the various ingredients added, and is therefore very filling and ideal as the first course when the main course is fairly light, or it can be a light meal in itself, particularly when followed by cheese and fresh fruit.

Shopping reminders:

Prawn chowder: prawns, can of tomato soup, cucumber.

Kidney dish: eggs, canned kidneys, bread or potatoes, port wine (optional), parsley; cabbage, salt, butter.

Dessert: can of creamed rice, oranges, jelly marmalade.

Menu:

Creamed spinach soup
Jamaican prawns with savoury potatoes
Ice cream with peppermint sauce

Creamed spinach soup

cooking time: 15 minutes

you will need for 4 servings:

large packet frozen chopped spinach (11–12 oz.)	½ pint milk
	½ pint water
1 oz. butter *or* margarine	1 chicken stock cube
1 oz. flour	seasoning

to serve:
croûtons of fried bread

1 Remove the spinach from the packet and break into one or two pieces if possible.
2 Heat the butter in a large pan.
3 Stir in the flour and cook for several minutes.
4 Gradually stir in the milk and water, bring to the boil and cook until smooth and thickened.
5 Add the stock cube and the pieces of frozen spinach and simmer steadily for approximately 10 minutes. Taste and season.
6 Serve in hot soup bowls with croûtons of fried bread, see page 76.

To vary:
Savoury spinach soup: fry 1 large chopped

onion in 2 oz. butter, proceed as above but use all chicken stock, or water and two chicken stock cubes. Top the spinach soup with a little cream or yoghourt or commercially soured cream and sprinkling of grated nutmeg.

Creamed asparagus soup: use large can asparagus tips instead of spinach and use the liquid in the can in place of some of the water – add chopped asparagus at stage 5.

Creamed mushroom soup: use 4 oz. mushrooms, cleaned and sliced finely, in place of a packet of frozen spinach.

Jamaican prawns

cooking time: 15 minutes

you will need for 4 servings:

2 oz. butter	2 tablespoons dry sherry or lemon juice
1 onion	
1 can condensed tomato soup	pinch cayenne pepper
6 oz. frozen shelled prawns (defrosted)*	pinch powdered cinnamon
1 green pepper	

to garnish:
little green pepper

*the best way to allow prawns to defrost is at room temperature or for a longer period in the cabinet of a refrigerator. If in a hurry, however, put the packet into a bowl of **cold** water.

1 Heat the butter in a large frying pan.
2 Peel and grate the onion and toss in the hot butter for approximately 5 minutes until tender but not brown.
3 Add the tomato soup and stir into the onion mixture.
4 Add all the rest of the ingredients, cutting the pepper into thin strips and putting some on one side for garnish.
5 Simmer gently for about 5 minutes, put into a hot serving dish and top with the pepper strips kept for garnish.

To vary:
Jamaican fish: use fingers of white fish or smoked haddock and simmer in the sauce at stage 5, for 10–12 minutes. Be sparing with salt if using smoked haddock.

Savoury potatoes

Buy a packet of dehydrated potatoes for 4 helpings, and heat as instructed on the packet. When the potatoes are smooth, add a good knob of butter or margarine, a shake of garlic salt, a little finely chopped parsley. Pile into a dish and top with paprika.

Ice cream with peppermint sauce

cooking time: few minutes

you will need for 4 servings:

block of vanilla ice cream or home-	made ice cream for 4 people. See page 87.

for sauce:

4 oz. peppermint creams	2 tablespoons top of the milk or thin cream
few drops green colouring	

1 Put the ice cream into serving glasses and top with hot or cold peppermint sauce.
2 Make the sauce by heating the ingredients in a basin over hot water until melted, then blend together.

To vary:

Chocolate peppermint sauce: use chocolate peppermint creams.

Marshmallow peppermint sauce: use 2 oz. marshmallows and 2 oz. peppermint creams.

Shopping reminders:

Soup: spinach, butter or margarine, flour, milk, chicken stock cube, salt and pepper, bread.

Fish, etc.: butter, onion, condensed tomato soup, prawns, green pepper, dry sherry or lemon juice, cayenne pepper, powdered cinnamon, dehydrated potatoes, garlic salt, parsley, paprika.

Dessert: ice cream, peppermint creams, green colouring, milk or thin cream.

Menu:
Cheese and carrot soup
Fish stuffed tomatoes with lettuce salad or green vegetable
Caramelled oranges with almonds

Cheese and carrot soup

cooking time: 15 minutes

you will need for 4 servings:

2 oz. butter or margarine	2 large carrots seasoning
1 oz. flour	2 oz. Cheddar cheese
1 pint milk	

1 Heat the butter in a saucepan.
2 Stir in the flour and cook for several minutes.
3 Gradually add the milk, bring to the boil and cook until you have a smooth thin sauce.
4 Add the coarsely grated, peeled carrots, simmer for 5 minutes, seasoning well.
5 Stir in the grated cheese and serve at once.

To vary:

Cheese and asparagus soup: add 2 oz. grated cheese to canned creamed asparagus soup.

Cheese and chicken soup: add 2 oz. grated cheese to canned cream of chicken soup.

Harlequin soup: add a small packet of frozen peas to the carrot etc., at stage 4, together with a chopped red pepper.

Fish stuffed tomatoes with lettuce salad or green vegetable

cooking time: 10–15 minutes

you will need for 4 servings:

8 medium tomatoes	½ oz. melted butter
2 oz. crisp bread-crumbs	seasoning
2 teaspoons finely chopped parsley	
1 teaspoon grated onion	
3–4 oz. shrimps or prawns*	**to garnish:**
or crab-meat	parsley
	1 lemon

*if frozen allow to defrost at room temperature

1 Cut tops off tomatoes and keep on one side.

2 To make stuffing, carefully scoop out inside of tomatoes and chop finely in a basin, mix with breadcrumbs, parsley, onion, whole shrimps, chopped prawns or flaked crab-meat, melted butter and seasoning.

3 Season the tomato cases lightly, pile in the stuffing, put on tomato tops, then stand on a lightly-greased shallow tin.

4 Heat towards the top of a moderately hot oven (400°F., Gas Mark 5–6) for 10–15 minutes.

5 Garnish with sprigs of parsley and twists of lemon.

To vary:

Chicken and ham tomatoes: use tiny pieces of left-over cooked chicken and ham in place of the fish.

Devilled tomatoes: use flaked white fish in place of shellfish. Add pinch cayenne pepper, curry powder, or a few drops Worcestershire sauce at stage 2.

Caramelled oranges with almonds

cooking time: 10 minutes

you will need for 4 servings:

4 large *or* 8 medium oranges	6 tablespoons water
3 oz. castor *or* granulated sugar	2 oz. blanched almonds

1 Cut the peel away from the oranges in such a way that you remove all the white pith.

2 Cut the oranges into thick slices and put into a shallow glass dish.

3 Stir the sugar and three tablespoons water in a strong saucepan over heat until the sugar has dissolved.

4 Boil steadily until a golden brown caramel.

5 Add the rest of the water, stir over a low heat until you have a pouring sauce, then spoon over the oranges.

6 Meanwhile brown the almonds under the grill and scatter over the caramel sauce.

To vary:

Caramelled apples: cut peeled, cored dessert apples in thick slices and poach for about 5 minutes in the syrup at stage 5.

Caramelled pears: use segments of fresh ripe pears instead of oranges.

Caramelled bananas: use thick slices of banana dipped in lemon juice in place of orange.

Shopping reminders:
Soup: butter, flour, milk, carrots, salt, pepper, Cheddar cheese.
Fish stuffed tomatoes: tomatoes, breadcrumbs, parsley, onion, shrimps, prawns or crab-meat, butter, salt, pepper, lemon.
Dessert: oranges, sugar, blanched almonds.

Menu:
Parmesan plaice with tomatoes, mushrooms and potato crisps
Orange bananas with butterscotch fritters

Orange bananas with butterscotch fritters

cooking time: 12–15 minutes

you will need for 4 servings:

3 oz. butter	2 large oranges
3 oz. brown sugar	4 bananas
4 thin fingers bread, without crusts	1 tablespoon brandy (optional)

1 Heat the butter in a strong frying pan.

2 Stir in the sugar and continue heating gently until the sugar has dissolved.

3 Put in the fingers of bread, turn in the butterscotch mixture until golden brown, then lift on to a hot serving dish.

4 Add the very finely grated rind and juice of the oranges to the butter and sugar remaining in the pan.

5 Put in the peeled, halved bananas and turn in the orange sauce, then simmer for approximately 5 minutes.

6 Lift the bananas on to the fritters and coat with any sauce remaining in the pan.

7 The brandy should be added at the last minute before removing the bananas.

To vary:

Pineapple bananas: as stages 1–3 above. Open a medium sized can of pineapple rings (this gives neater shaped pieces than pineapple cubes). Cut the fruit into strips and put into the frying pan with the liquid from the can, at stage 4, omitting oranges. Continue as stages 5–7.

Coconut bananas: use either oranges or pineapple. Sprinkle 1–2 oz. freshly grated coconut or desiccated coconut over the bananas just before serving.

Parmesan plaice with tomatoes, mushrooms and potato crisps

cooking time: 10–15 minutes

you will need for 4 servings:

4 large fillets plaice*	seasoning
1 oz. margarine *or* butter	1 oz. crisp bread-crumbs (raspings)
	1 oz. grated Parmesan cheese
to garnish:	
1 lemon	watercress
to serve:	
4 tomatoes	2–3 packets potato crisps
4 oz. mushrooms	

*these may be fresh or frozen, and frozen plaice fillets may be cooked without defrosting, but allow a little longer in cooking

1 Wash and dry the fish and put on the greased grid of the grill pan.
2 Brush with most of the melted margarine or butter.
3 Season lightly and cook for approximately 4–5 minutes under a pre-heated grill.
4 Remove, sprinkle the top of each fillet with the crumbs and the Parmesan cheese.
5 Return to the grill and cook for a few minutes only.
6 Garnish with lemon and watercress and serve with fried or grilled tomatoes and fried or grilled mushrooms and heated potato crisps.

Note: to *fry* the tomatoes and mushrooms you need a little extra fat; to *grill* the tomatoes and mushrooms, heat about 1 oz. margarine or butter in the grill pan itself, put the vegetables into the grill pan, cook until nearly tender then put the plaice on the grid and continue as above.

To vary:
Obviously other fish may be used instead of plaice.
Cheddar plaice: use 2 oz. grated Cheddar in place of Parmesan cheese.
Lemon plaice: omit the cheese, blend the grated rind of 1 lemon with the crumbs at stage 4, and sprinkle with the lemon juice.

Shopping reminders:
Fish: plaice, margarine or butter, salt, pepper, breadcrumbs, Parmesan cheese, lemon, watercress, tomatoes, mushrooms, potato crisps.
Dessert: butter, brown sugar, bread, oranges, bananas, brandy (optional).

Menu:
Chilled mulligatawny soup with almond garnish.
Fish meunière with sprigged cauliflower and new potatoes
Ice cream with chocolate sauce

Fish meunière with sprigged cauliflower and new potatoes

Buy frozen or fresh fish – this can be plaice fillets, sole fillets, trout, cutlets of cod or other white fish. If buying frozen fish, buy the *non-coated* fish.

cooking time: 10–15 minutes

you will need for 4 servings:

4 cutlets fish, whole fish or large fillets (see above)	juice of 1 lemon *or* 1 tablespoon vinegar
seasoning	1 tablespoon chopped parsley
2–3 oz. butter (a little more may be necessary)	2 teaspoons capers

1 Wash and dry the fish well, do not coat but season lightly.
2 Heat the butter in a frying pan and fry the fish in this until just tender; time depends on the fish used.
3 Lift on to a hot dish and keep warm. If no butter is left in the pan then add another 1–2 oz.
4 Heat the butter until it becomes golden coloured, then add the rest of the ingredients

and pour over the fish. This is an excellent way of frying fish without the bother of coating it first, or making a sauce.

5 Serve with the cooked sprigged cauliflower, and potatoes garnished with chopped parsley.

To vary:

Fried fish: coat the fish in seasoned flour then in beaten egg, diluted with a very little water if wished, and crisp breadcrumbs (raspings), or buy ready-coated frozen fish. Either fry in shallow fat or enough oil to give a good coating at the bottom of the pan, or in deep fat or oil. Test that this is hot enough to turn a cube of day-old bread golden coloured within 1 minute before lowering the fish into the pan. Instead of egg and crumbs the fish may be coated in a batter (only suitable if you intend to use deep fat). To make this, blend batter as page 53 but use a little less liquid, so this sticks to the fish, which should be given a very thin coating of seasoned flour first. Turn the fish on to second side if frying in shallow fat, but if using deep fat the fish browns all over and needs no turning.

Always drain the fried fish on absorbent paper before serving and garnish with lemon and parsley.

5 easy ways to vary the flavour of fried fish

Savoury coating:
Buy packet stuffing – parsley and thyme or sage and onion – and coat the fish fillets with beaten egg and the dry stuffing instead of breadcrumbs; this gives a most interesting taste.

Tomato coating:
Mix an egg yolk with tomato juice and coat the fish with this instead of plain egg.

Cheese coating:
Blend equal quantities of finely grated cheese and raspings together to coat the fish. (This is not suitable for very thick cutlets of fish or whole fish, as the frying time will be too long and could cause the cheese to become tough.)

Curried fried fish:
Blend a little curry powder with the raspings in which you coat the fish; for a strong flavour blend curry powder with the beaten egg as well.

Lemon meunière:
Use the basic recipe for Fish meunière, page

36, but instead of parsley and capers flavour the browned butter with finely chopped cucumber, or gherkins and pieces of lemon instead of lemon juice.

Grilled fish: brush the grid of the grill pan with a little melted butter or fat, this prevents the fish 'sticking' to the grid. Brush the fish with melted butter or fat, season, and cook under a hot grill. If cooking thick fillets or cutlets of fish or whole fish you must turn the fish during cooking; thin fillets do not need turning. Always keep the fish well 'basted' with butter or fat as it cooks.

5 easy ways to vary the flavour of grilled fish

Orange fish:
Most white fish is delicious if given an orange flavour while being grilled. Blend very finely grated orange rind with the melted butter or fat, use this for basting the fish as it cooks. Squeeze orange juice over the fish when nearly cooked. Garnish with wedges of orange and parsley.

Fish Milanaise:
Chop 1 onion and 3 tomatoes very thinly and blend with the melted butter or fat. Use this for basting the fish as it cooks.

Herbed grilled fish:
Blend freshly chopped parsley, thyme and sage with the melted butter or fat used in basting.

Marinated fish:
Blend $\frac{1}{4}$ pint white wine with a finely chopped onion, 2 tablespoons olive oil, seasoning and a few chopped fresh herbs. Put the fish in this for 1 hour before cooking, turning from time to time, then grill the fish. You need no extra fat, as the oil keeps the fish moist. Any marinade left may be poured over the fish just before it has finished cooking.

Grilled fish au gratin:
Grill the fish on one side in the usual way. Turn and brush with melted butter, then grill for 2–3 minutes. Remove from under the grill and top with grated cheese and fine soft breadcrumbs and a little melted butter, grill until a golden brown crust forms.
If using thin fillets of fish, grill for 2–3 minutes, do not turn but put on the topping and proceed as above.

Ice cream and chocolate sauce

cooking time: few minutes

you will need for 4 servings:

large block ice
   cream

for the sauce:

4 oz. plain chocolate	1 tablespoon water
	½ oz. butter

1 Keep the ice cream firm in the freezing compartment of the refrigerator or in a thick wrapping of newspaper.
2 To make the sauce: break the chocolate into pieces and put with the water and butter in a basin over a saucepan of very hot water. Leave until melted, stir and serve hot.

To vary:

Mocha sauce: use coffee essence instead of water.

Orange chocolate sauce: add the finely grated rind of 1 orange to the chocolate and use 1 tablespoon orange juice. If wished, tiny pieces of fresh orange pulp may be put on the ice cream before topping with the sauce.

Chocolate brandy sauce: use brandy instead of water.

To serve the sauce cold: since the sauce stiffens as it cools, you should add 2 tablespoons water or other liquid when stirring, and allow to cool.

Chilled mulligatawny soup

Open a medium sized can of the soup and blend with an equal amount of cold milk. Put into soup cups and top with a few blanched almonds.
Obviously the soup can be served hot, diluted with stock, water or milk.

Note: If you are serving the soup cold you need more cold liquid than when it is to be served heated.

Shopping reminders:

Soup: canned mulligatawny soup, milk, almonds.

Fish meunière: fish, butter, lemon or vinegar, parsley, capers, cauliflower, potatoes (fresh or canned), salt, pepper.
Dessert: ice cream, chocolate, butter.

Menu:
**Grilled chops with tomatoes,
  mushrooms and chipped potatoes
Almond Alaska
Cheese and biscuits**

Chipped potatoes

These can be fried in shallow fat, although they are much better if cooked in deep fat or oil.
If using fresh potatoes: peel, cut into slices about 1/3rd inch thick, then into narrow fingers, i.e. chips (or use a proper chip cutter). Dry the potatoes well. If using frozen chips use straight from the packet, do not defrost.
For shallow fat: Heat enough fat or oil to give about ½ inch in the frying pan, fry the potatoes until golden brown on the underside, turn and fry on the second side. If wished, the potatoes may be lifted out, the fat reheated and the potatoes fried again as for deep fat.
For deep fat: Heat the fat or oil to 350° F. or until a cube of day-old bread will turn golden-coloured within 1 minute. Dry the potatoes well and put into a frying basket, lower into the hot oil or fat. *Never have the basket more than half-filled.* Fry steadily until the potatoes are tender, do not try to get them very brown. If frying lots of potatoes, cook the second and third batches in the same way. Put on to a dish or plate. Reheat the oil or fat to a higher temperature – until a cube of bread turns golden in about ½ minute – lower the chips into this and fry very quickly until crisp and golden brown. Always drain on absorbent paper. Sprinkle with a little salt before serving, if wished.

Grilled chops with tomatoes and mushrooms

Veal chops: add a little fat over the lean part.

Pork chops: cut away the rind and snip the fat at regular intervals to encourage this to become crisp.
Lamb chops: need little if any fat.

Put the halved tomatoes and washed and dried mushrooms into the grill pan, top them with seasoning and a little butter or margarine. Place under the hot grill for a few moments to start the cooking process, then put the chops on the grid over the vegetables, and continue as page 41.

Almond Alaska

cooking time: 2–3 minutes

you will need for 4 servings:

1 block ice cream	3 oz. castor sugar
1 medium can apricots *or* other fruit	2 oz. blanched almonds, whole
3 egg whites	

1 Put the ice cream in an ovenproof dish.
2 Place the well-drained apricots round.
3 Whisk the egg whites until very stiff, gradually whisk in the sugar.
4 Pile over the ice cream and top with nuts.
5 Put for 2–3 minutes under the grill until brown. (Do this just after dishing up the chops and before serving them.)
6 Put the Alaska on one side and it will be quite all right to serve this after you have eaten your main course.

To vary:
Baked Alaska: recipe as above, or put the ice cream and fruit on a sponge base. Top with meringue and bake for 3–5 minutes in a very hot oven (475–500° F., Gas Mark 9–10).
Note: as heat is all round the ice cream in the oven, you will need 4 egg whites and 4 oz. sugar *at least*.
Chocolate Alaska: use a chocolate sponge and ice cream as the basis of the dessert.
Coconut Alaska: use any fruit with the ice cream. Make the meringue, but fold 1½–2 oz. desiccated coconut into the egg whites with the sugar.
Coffee Alaska: moisten a plain sponge with strong sweetened coffee flavoured with rum or

Tia Maria – top with vanilla or coffee ice cream and pears, then the meringue.
Mincemeat Alaska: moisten a sponge with brandy, top with mincemeat, ice cream and meringue.
Strawberry Alaska: use strawberry ice cream and sliced or whole strawberries. Of course other fruits and ice creams may be chosen.

Note: In all these variations you can use either grill or oven.

Shopping reminders:
Chops, etc.: chops,* tomatoes, mushrooms, butter or other fat, seasoning, potatoes, fat or oil for frying.
Dessert: ice cream, canned apricots, eggs, sugar, almonds.
Cheese: selection of cheese (see page 85), biscuits, butter – watercress and/or celery when in season.

*When buying lamb ask for best end of neck or loin chops.
When buying pork ask for loin chops.
When buying veal ask for loin chops.

Menu:
Melon
Fried chops with fried cucumber and tomato pepper salad
Banana custard

Banana custard

Make 1 pint of custard, but use just a little more than usual so that it is fairly thick. Sweeten well and add the finely grated rind of 1 orange or lemon if wished. Slice 4 firm bananas into 4 serving dishes, top with a sprinkling of lemon juice to keep the fruit white, then top with the custard. Decorate with chopped nuts or whipped cream if wished.

Fried chops with fried cucumber

Follow directions for frying chops as page 40.

Lift on to a hot dish and keep warm. Peel the cucumber if wished, but the peel gives flavour if not too thick and tough. Coat the slices of cucumber with seasoned flour and fry in hot fat in the frying pan until crisp and golden brown.

8 new ways to serve chops or cutlets

Chops and cutlets are quick to cook and therefore ideal for the busy working housewife.

To fry: Use a little fat in the pan for very lean lamb chops or cutlets, rather more for veal, no fat for pork or fat lamb. Heat the fat and fry the meat quickly on either side (to seal in the flavour) then lower the heat and cook more slowly until tender.

To grill: Pre-heat the grill, brush lean meat (see above) with a little fat. Grill quickly on either side to seal in the flavour then lower the heat of the grill, or move the grill pan further away from the heat and cook more slowly and gently until the meat is tender.

Ways to give new flavour

(quantities are for 4 chops or equivalent)

À la Portugaise: fry 1–2 finely chopped onions in 2 oz. fat until tender, add meat and fry for several minutes, then add 4–6 skinned chopped tomatoes and 8 tablespoons (¼ pint) water or white wine. Season well adding a pinch of garlic salt. Cook gently, turning meat once or twice, for about 15 minutes. If wished a lid can be placed on the pan to make sure the mixture does not become dry – excellent with veal or pork.

With soured cream: cook meat and lift out of pan. Add ¼ pint dairy soured cream* and 1 teaspoon capers. Heat gently then pour over the meat.

Excellent with all meats – but *not* with fat pork.
*or ¼ pint thin cream and 1 tablespoon lemon juice.

In paprika sauce: cook meat in the frying pan, lift out. Blend 1–2 teaspoons paprika and 1 teaspoon cornflour with ¼ pint tomato juice. Put into frying pan and heat for a few minutes, stirring well. Pour over meat and top with twists of lemon.

Particularly good with veal or pork.

In onion sauce: grate or chop 2 onions finely or use 1 tablespoon dehydrated onion (soaked in 3 tablespoons cold water for 10 minutes). Fry the meat, then lift out of pan. Toss the onions in the fat remaining in the pan for 5 minutes. Blend ½ oz. cornflour with ½ pint brown stock (or use canned consommé, or water and ½ or 1 beef stock cube). Add to the onion mixture, bring to the boil, cook until thickened, flavour with

a) few drops Worcestershire sauce and squeeze lemon juice, *or*

b) 1 tablespoon concentrated tomato purée, *or*

c) Add 1 tablespoon chopped pickled walnuts and ½ tablespoon sliced olives.

Suitable for all meals.

In Burgundy sauce: follow directions for onion sauce but use a red Burgundy instead of stock. Particularly good with lamb or pork.

In cucumber yoghourt: cook the meat in a frying pan, lift out. Add 2 cartons plain yoghourt and 3 tablespoons thin strips of peeled cucumber. Heat gently and serve with the meat. Delicious with lamb or veal.

Curried chops: coat the meat in a little flour mixed with curry powder. Fry or grill as usual – good for all meats.

Au poivre: crush a few peppercorns, press into both sides of the uncooked meat and fry in the usual way. Excellent with all meats, although veal is nicer if you make a sauce as for steak au poivre (see page 41).

Au gratin: grill the meat as usual quickly on both sides, then remove from under the grill. Sprinkle one side of the meat with finely grated cheese, breadcrumbs and dot with butter. Put under grill again and cook steadily until the meat is tender. Excellent with veal or lamb.

Tomato pepper salad

Arrange thinly sliced tomatoes and rings of green or red pepper on a bed of lettuce, top with a dressing made with a little oil, vinegar and seasoning.

Shopping reminders:
Melon: melon, sugar, ginger.
Fried chops, etc.: chops, fat, cucumber, flour,

salt, pepper, tomatoes, green or red pepper, oil, vinegar, lettuce.

Dessert: custard powder, milk, sugar, lemon, bananas, nuts and cream (optional).

Grapefruit and orange cocktail

Follow directions on page 20, put in a cold place to chill. A little sherry may be added if wished.

Grilled steak with grilled tomatoes, mushrooms and green salad

Make the green salad first but do not put any oil and vinegar on it until ready to serve.

Make the parsley butter: for 4 pats: cream 2 oz. butter with a good squeeze lemon juice, add 1 tablespoon parsley, chopped finely. Form into a neat shape, then cut into pats and chill. (This could be done beforehand if wished.)

Prepare the grill:
Halve the tomatoes and put these and the washed and dried mushrooms into the grill pan. Top with a little butter and seasoning. Cook for about 5 minutes under the grill, a little longer if the steak is to be very under-done. Put the 4 portions of steak on the grid, top with a generous amount of butter, season if wished.

For a really underdone steak, cook for 2–3 minutes, turn and cook for the same time on the second side, then serve.
A very thin minute steak would need just 1 minute on either side to be underdone.

A medium-cooked steak – time as above,

lower the heat and/or move the grill pan further away from the heat and cook for a further 3–4 minutes.

A very well-done steak – cook as under-done steak, then lower the heat and/or move the grill pan further away from the heat and cook for a further 5–6 minutes, basting well during this time with butter so that it does not become too dry.

To serve: arrange steaks, tomatoes, mushrooms on the hot dish, put the parsley butter (often called maître d'hôtel butter) on each steak before serving.

To vary grilled steak

Fried steak: heat a little butter in the pan and fry the steak on either side, then lower heat and time as for grilled steak.

Herbed steaks: press finely chopped fresh herbs into each side of the steaks before frying or grilling.

Marinated steaks: this is particularly useful if you are not sure the steaks are as tender as you would wish. Make a marinade of $\frac{1}{4}$ pint cheap red wine, 2–3 tablespoons olive oil, 1 chopped clove or crushed clove of garlic, seasoning. Put into a shallow dish and lay the steaks on this, turn once or twice and leave for about 1 hour, at least, before cooking.

Peppered steak or steak au poivre: crush peppercorns with a rolling pin and press into both sides of the uncooked steak. Fry in hot butter until cooked as wished.

Peppered steak with cream sauce: recipe as peppered steak, when the meat is cooked lift from the pan on to a hot dish, then add about $\frac{1}{4}$ pint thin cream and 1–2 tablespoons brandy to the meat juices, and heat through gently and slowly. Pour over the steaks and garnish with chopped parsley.

Steak chasseur: make a purée of 4 skinned chopped tomatoes, 1 very finely chopped or grated onion, seasoning. Fry the steaks in the pan; when nearly cooked add the purée and continue cooking until tender.

Steak Diane: choose thin slices of rump steak, i.e. minute steaks. Fry a very finely chopped onion in the pan (or 2 onions if small) in plenty of butter, then add the 4 steaks, with seasoning, a little chopped parsley, a little Worcestershire

41

sauce and a little brandy, and cook until tender. If a browner outside to the steaks is preferred, fry the steaks first in butter, then lift on to a hot dish, add onions, etc. to pan and cook for a few minutes, then pour over the steaks.

Tournedos with pâté: buy fillet steaks and ask the butcher to tie them into rounds, or do this yourself. Fry or grill, put on to rounds of fried bread, topped with pâté, and garnish each tournedo with a neat pat of pâté; other garnishes may be used.

Shopping reminders:

Grapefruit and orange cocktail: grapefruit, oranges, sugar, sherry (optional).

Grilled steak, etc.: steaks (choose fillet, rump, sirloin – these are the most usual, although there are others which the butcher will show you), butter, tomatoes, mushrooms, lettuce, watercress, celery (optional), green pepper (optional), oil, vinegar, seasoning, parsley, lemon.

Cheese, etc.: either cheese, biscuits, butter, or ingredients for tarts as page 83.

Menu:
Anchovy eggs with salad
Sausage Jambalaya
   with cauliflower au gratin
Apple crunch

Apple crunch

cooking time: 25 minutes

you will need for 4 servings:

medium can apple
   sauce

for the topping:

2 oz. margarine	2 oz. golden syrup
2 oz. brown sugar	4 oz. crushed cornflakes

1 Put the apple sauce into a heatproof dish.
2 Blend the margarine, sugar, syrup and cornflakes together.
3 Spread over the top of the apple sauce.

4 Bake for 20–25 minutes, towards the top of a moderate to moderately hot oven (375–400°F., Gas Mark 4–5).

To vary:

Apple flapjack: use rolled oats instead of cornflakes, but bake for approximately 40 minutes in the centre of a very moderate to moderate oven (350–375°F., Gas Mark 3–4).

Chocolate crunch: excellent on sliced, well drained canned pears – as apple crunch, but blend 1 oz. sieved cocoa with the other ingredients.

Coconut crunch: use 3 oz. cornflakes and 2 oz. desiccated coconut – very good on rhubarb as well as apple. If using fresh rhubarb cut into pieces, put in the dish with sugar to taste, but only about 1 tablespoon water or orange juice.

Anchovy eggs

Hard-boil and halve 4 eggs, remove the yolks and blend with 1 oz. butter, 1–2 teaspoons anchovy essence. Pile back into the halved egg white cases. Put on to a bed of green salad.

To vary:

Asparagus eggs: blend the egg yolk with a little mayonnaise and chopped asparagus tips. Arrange the filled egg halves on salad garnished with more asparagus tips.

Corn eggs: blend the yolks with a little butter, grated Parmesan cheese and canned sweetcorn. Pile filling in the egg white cases, place on a bed of lettuce and garnish with sliced tomatoes topped with more corn.

Devilled eggs: blend the egg yolks with curry powder, a little chutney, Worcestershire sauce and a small amount of butter. Pile back into the egg white cases and serve on a green or rice salad, see pages 49 and 86.

Ham eggs: blend the egg yolks with butter or mayonnaise and finely chopped cooked ham. Pile back into the egg white cases and top with strips of green pepper.

Salmon eggs: blend the egg yolks with flaked canned or fresh cooked salmon and mayonnaise. Fill cases and serve on a bed of lettuce and sliced cucumber.

Sausage Jambalaya

cooking time: 20 minutes

you will need for 4 servings:

1 lb. pork *or* beef
  sausages
2 onions
1 can concentrated
  tomato soup

1 medium can beans
  in tomato sauce

to garnish:

chopped parsley *or*
  green pepper

1 Cut the sausages into ½–1 inch lengths.
2 Fry in a frying pan for a few minutes until brown on the outside.
3 Peel and grate the onions and add to the sausages, together with other ingredients (seasoning should not be necessary), simmer for 10–12 minutes.
4 Top with parsley or strips of pepper just before serving.

Cauliflower au gratin

Trim and divide the cauliflower into small flowerets and cook until just tender, top with grated cheese and crisp breadcrumbs. Heat under the grill for 2–3 minutes, if wished.

To vary Jambalaya: omit the beans and add sliced cooked potatoes to the tomato mixture. Use mulligatawny soup instead of tomato soup and stir in 2 oz. cooked rice instead of the beans.

Use canned mushroom soup instead of tomato soup and add a small can of sweetcorn to the mixture.

Shopping reminders:

Anchovy eggs: eggs, butter, anchovy essence, lettuce, watercress, etc.
Jambalaya: sausages, onions, concentrated tomato soup, canned beans in tomato sauce, parsley or green pepper. Cauliflower, cheese, breadcrumbs.
Dessert: Canned apple sauce, margarine, brown sugar, golden syrup, cornflakes.

Menu:
**Ham and tongue omelette with
  tomato purée and fried cucumber
Raspberry flan**

Raspberry flan [F]

no cooking

you will need for 4 servings:

for the flan:
2 oz. butter
2 oz. castor sugar

2 teaspoons golden
  syrup
4 oz. cornflakes

for the filling:
large packet frozen
  raspberries (8–10 oz.)

1 Cream the butter, sugar and golden syrup.
2 Add the crushed cornflakes (the best way to crush these is either by rolling between 2 sheets of greaseproof paper, or just with your hands in a large bowl).
3 Press into a flan shape and leave to set for about 1 hour.
4 Meanwhile, allow the raspberries to defrost – *never over-defrost frozen fruit.*
5 Drain and lift into the flan case, serve the syrup separately.
Note: Some raspberries are frozen without sugar, and this means adding sugar to them as they defrost.

To vary:

Raspberry cream filling [F] – whip ¼ pint thick cream until it just holds its shape. Fold in the well-drained raspberries and sweeten to taste. Pile into the flan case.
With fresh fruit – buy 1–1¼ lb. fresh raspberries. Mash approximately 4 oz., sweeten and spread over the bottom of the flan. Top with whole sweetened fruit. Serve with cream.

Tomato purée

Tip a medium sized can of peeled tomatoes into a saucepan, season well, add a little garlic salt and chopped parsley if wished. Serve in a sauce-boat.

Fried cucumber

Peel the cucumber and cut into ¼-inch slices. Coat in seasoned flour and fry in hot fat until crisp and golden brown on both sides. Lower the heat and cook for a few minutes.

Ham and tongue omelette with tomato purée and fried cucumber

cooking time: 8 minutes

you will need for 4 servings:

3 oz. cooked ham
3 oz. cooked tongue
2 oz. butter

6 eggs
seasoning

to garnish:

chopped parsley

to serve:

tomato purée   fried cucumber

Note: If possible make 2 omelettes rather than 1 very large one, for if the mixture is too thick the omelette takes longer to cook and is dry.

1 Cut the ham and tongue into thin strips.
2 Heat the butter in a large omelette pan and toss the meat in this for approximately 1 minute.
3 Beat the eggs with the seasoning, do not over-salt.
4 Pour over the ham and tongue and cook in the usual way, see page 20.
5 Fold and serve at once garnished with chopped parsley.

To vary:

Bacon and tomato omelette: fry chopped bacon instead of ham and tongue. Fill omelette with sliced tomatoes.

Cheese omelette: add 3–4 oz. grated cheese to the beaten eggs.

Chicken and corn omelette: toss 4 oz. cooked chicken and 2 oz. drained canned corn in the butter, at stage 2.

Fish omelette: add 2–4 oz. chopped prawns to the beaten eggs, or use flaked crab-meat. White fish, blended with a white sauce, makes an excellent filling for an omelette.

Potato omelette: heat sliced potatoes in the butter, at stage 2.

Mushroom omelette: fry 2–3 oz. sliced mushrooms in the butter, at stage 2.

Shopping reminders:

Omelette: ham, tongue, butter, eggs, salt, pepper, parsley, can of peeled tomatoes, garlic salt, cucumber, flour.

Dessert: butter, castor sugar, golden syrup, cornflakes, frozen raspberries.

Menu:
Gammon steaks with stuffed tomatoes, creamed potatoes, peas
Banana apricot fritters

Gammon steaks with stuffed tomatoes, creamed potatoes and peas

cooking time: 15–20 minutes

you will need for 4 servings:

4 slices gammon
1 oz. butter
4 large tomatoes
½ tablespoon
  chopped gherkins

½ tablespoon
  chopped cocktail
  onions
seasoning

to garnish:

watercress

to serve:

creamed potatoes,
  peas

1 Remove skin from the gammon and snip the fat at regular intervals so that the fat does not curl.
2 Spread lean part of the gammon with the butter.
3 Halve the tomatoes, scoop out the pulp, mix with the gherkins, onions and seasoning and pack into the seasoned tomato cases.
4 Put the halved tomatoes into grill pan, cook for 5 minutes under a hot grill (unless you are sure the tomatoes will cook *with* the bacon). Keep warm.
5 Put the gammon slices on the grid of the grill pan and cook for 10–15 minutes (according to thickness of the bacon).

6 Arrange on a hot dish with the tomatoes and watercress. Serve with creamed potatoes and peas.

To vary:

Use thick back rashers (often called bacon chops) instead of gammon rashers.

Omit stuffed tomatoes and heat rings of canned pineapple (brushed with a little melted butter) under the grill for a few minutes.

Baste the gammon rashers with a little red wine while cooking.

Banana apricot 'fritters'

cooking time: 5–6 minutes

you will need for 4 servings:

8 large slices bread	1 egg
3 oz. butter	4 tablespoons milk
2 bananas	3 tablespoons water
5 tablespoons apricot jam	

1 Spread the bread with 1 oz. butter.

2 Mash bananas with 1–2 tablespoons apricot jam.

3 Make sandwiches with the banana and jam mixture and cut them into fingers (removing crusts).

4 Beat egg and milk and dip sandwich fingers in this mixture.

5 Fry in the hot butter until crisp and brown on either side.

6 Serve on a hot dish topped with apricot sauce, made by heating the jam and water.

To vary:

Use all jam and omit bananas.

Shopping reminders:

Gammon dish: gammon, butter, tomatoes, gherkins, cocktail onions, salt, pepper, watercress.

Vegetables: potatoes (little butter or margarine and milk to cream), peas, salt, pepper.

Dessert: bread, butter, bananas, apricot jam, egg, milk.

Menu:
Melon
Gammon Florentine
Ice cream and fudge sauce

Ice cream and fudge sauce

cooking time: few minutes

you will need for 4 servings:

for the sauce:

¼ pint milk	large block ice cream
4 oz. fudge	

1 Put the milk and fudge into a basin and stand basin over boiling water.

2 Heat until the fudge has melted, blend, then allow to cool so that mixture stiffens slightly.

3 Pour over the ice cream.

Gammon Florentine

cooking time: 15 minutes*

you will need for 4 servings:

4 thick slices gammon	approx. 2 lb. fresh spinach *or* equivalent in frozen spinach
1 oz. melted butter	
3 teaspoons made-mustard	
½–1 tablespoon brown sugar	1 oz. butter
4 tomatoes	little top of milk *or* cream
	seasoning

*this will be a little more if using fresh spinach

1 Remove the rind from the gammon, snip the edges of the fat so it will crisp.

2 Do not pre-heat the grill – gammon is better if put under a cold grill to prevent the edges curling.

3 Brush the lean with a little melted butter and cook for about 5–6 minutes.

4 While the gammon is cooking, blend the rest of the butter with the mustard and sugar, turn the gammon and spread this over the other side.

5 Cook fairly quickly until the fat begins to brown lightly, then lower the heat under the grill and continue cooking for 5–10 minutes, (depending on the thickness of the gammon) and adding the tomatoes a few minutes before the end of the cooking time.

6 Meanwhile cook the spinach, drain, blend with the butter, cream and seasoning.

7 Arrange on a hot dish topped with the gammon and tomatoes.

Melon, sugar.
Gammon Florentine: gammon, butter, mustard, brown sugar, tomatoes, spinach, thin cream or milk, seasoning.
Dessert: ice cream, fudge, milk.

Menu:
Grapefruit
Barbecued beef, savoury rice, creamed spinach
Saucer pancakes

Barbecued beef

cooking time: 15–30 minutes

you will need for 4 servings:

2 oz. butter	pinch curry powder
4 fillets beef *or*	pinch chilli powder
portions rump	*or* teaspoon chilli
steak	sauce
seasoning	few drops
1 onion	Worcestershire
4 skinned tomatoes	sauce

1 Spread half the butter over dish, arrange steak on this.
2 Spread rest of butter on steaks.
3 Mix plenty of seasoning, the grated onion, chopped tomatoes, and other ingredients together.
4 Top the steaks with this and cover with foil.
5 Allow 15 minutes for underdone steak, 20 for medium cooked, and up to 30 minutes for very well done steak, in the centre of a hot oven (425° F., Gas Mark 6).

To vary:
Use thick slices corned beef and heat for 10–15 minutes.
Choose lamb chops instead of beef.

Savoury rice

cooking time: 18–20 minutes*

you will need for 4 servings:

4 oz. long grain rice	2 oz. sultanas

8 fl. oz. (nearly ½ pint) stock *or* water and ½ stock cube   seasoning

*unless using 'instant' rice.

1 Put rice and cold stock into a saucepan and bring to the boil.
2 Stir briskly with a fork, cover the pan lightly, *simmer* for 10 minutes over a low heat.
3 Add sultanas, cover and leave over low heat for a further 5 minutes. By this time the rice should be tender and all the liquid absorbed. Season well.

To vary:
Use water instead of stock. Omit the sultanas, add 1 finely chopped green pepper.
Add 1 oz. sultanas and 1 oz. shredded fresh coconut instead of all sultanas.

Creamed spinach

Cook frozen or fresh spinach, drain well, return to the pan with a little thick cream and reheat.

Saucer pancakes

cooking time: 20 minutes

you will need for 4–5 servings:

2 oz. margarine *or*	2 oz. flour
butter	¼ pint milk
2 oz. sugar	little extra butter
2 eggs	*or* oil
	jam

1 Cream margarine and sugar until soft.
2 Gradually beat in eggs, the flour, and lastly the milk – the mixture will curdle slightly but that does not matter.
3 Grease saucers or plates – these should be large and flat – ovenproof glassware is excellent – and heat in oven for 5 minutes, do this just before dishing up first course.
4 Pour batter into saucers and cook for 15 minutes just above centre of a moderately hot to hot oven (375–400°F., Gas Mark 5–6).
5 Top with jam and serve at once in the saucers, or lift on to another serving dish.

To vary:

A pleasant texture is given if 1 oz. flour and 1 oz. semolina is used, instead of all flour. Serve the hot pancakes with hot thick fruit purée and ice cream instead of jam.
Serve the hot pancakes with ice cream and hot chocolate sauce.

Shopping reminders:

Grapefruit, sugar
Barbecued beef: fillet or rump steak, butter, salt and pepper, onion, tomatoes, curry powder, chilli powder or sauce, Worcestershire sauce.
Savoury rice: long grain rice, stock or stock cube, sultanas, salt and pepper. Vegetables: spinach.
Pancakes: margarine or butter, sugar, eggs, flour, milk, extra butter or oil, jam.

Menu:
Meat fritters with Duchesse potatoes
Fruit snow

Fruit snow

no cooking

you will need for 4 servings:

¾–1 pint very thick sweetened fruit purée (apples, plums, rhubarb, etc.) or sieved fruit pie filling or canned apple sauce

2 egg whites

to decorate:

4 glacé cherries

1 Put fruit purée into basin.
2 Whisk egg whites until very stiff.
3 Fold into the fruit mixture carefully, to give a fluffy texture.
4 Serve in glasses topped with a glacé cherry.

To vary:

Frosted snow: freeze for about 30 minutes until lightly iced.
Cream snow: (or quick mousse) – add ¼ pint whipped thick cream to the fruit *before* adding egg white.
Nutty snow: add 2–3 oz. chopped nuts (walnuts, blanched almonds, hazel nuts, as desired) to fruit purée.

Duchesse potatoes

To save time use a packet of dehydrated potatoes and prepare as directions, add a little extra margarine or butter and beat in 2 egg yolks (to make enough potato for 4 people). Pipe or pile this round the edge of an ovenproof dish and brown under a hot grill or in the oven for a short time. Arrange the fritters, etc. in the centre of the potato border.

Meat fritters

cooking time: 10 minutes

you will need for 4 servings:

8–10 oz. cooked meat*

for the batter:	to fry:
4 oz. self-raising flour	(deep or shallow) fat
pinch salt	
shake of mixed herbs	**to garnish:**
pinch of curry powder (optional)	4 tomatoes
1 teaspoon horse-radish sauce (optional)	bunch watercress
1 egg	
¼ pint milk	
4 tablespoons water	

*corned beef, cooked ham, cooked tongue or other cooked meats are suitable.

1 Cut cooked meat into neat pieces, or flake corned beef.
2 Mix all the ingredients for the batter together, then blend in the meat. Heat the fat and put spoonfuls of the mixture into this.
3 Fry steadily on either side until crisp and golden brown. If using deep fat, leave for 1–2 minutes longer to make certain the mixture is cooked right through; with shallow fat you need to cook for a further 5 minutes.
4 Drain on absorbent paper and garnish with fresh or grilled tomatoes and watercress.

To vary:

Beef and tomato puffs: use bottled tomato juice in place of milk and water. This is particularly suitable with flaked corned beef.

Shopping reminders:

Meat fritters: cooked meat, self-raising flour, salt, mixed herbs, curry powder (optional), horseradish sauce (optional), egg, milk, fat, tomatoes, watercress, packet dehydrated potatoes, margarine or butter, 2 eggs.

Dessert: cooked fruit or canned fruit or pie filling or sauce, egg whites, glacé cherries.

Menu:
Orange liver slices, new potatoes, peas
Sponge castle puddings

Sponge castle puddings

This recipe is a basic one which indicates the modern method of one-stage mixing with the new softened margarines. Use the same recipe for large puddings too.

cooking time: 15 minutes

you will need for 4 servings:

3½ oz. luxury type margarine	4 oz. self raising flour
3 oz. castor sugar	3–4 tablespoons jam
2 small eggs	*or* golden syrup

1 Use nearly ½ oz. of the margarine to grease small castle pudding (dariole) tins; save a little for greasing the paper or foil.
2 Cream together the margarine, sugar, eggs and flour for 2–3 minutes until blended.
3 Divide the jam between the 8 dariole tins.
4 Cover with the mixture (if the tins are rather small you may need 12, since there must be room for the mixture to rise).
5 Cover with greased paper or foil and screw this round the top.
6 Stand the small tins in a steamer over a pan of boiling water and cook for 15–20 minutes or until firm.
7 Turn out and serve with one of the sauces mentioned on page 53.

Orange liver slices with new potatoes and peas

cooking time: 15 minutes

you will need for 4 servings:

1 lb. lambs' *or* calves' liver	2–3 oz. butter *or* margarine
2 large oranges	seasoning

to garnish:

1 orange	little chopped parsley

1 Cut the liver into thin slices if not already done by the butcher.
2 Grate the rind of the oranges finely, using only the top 'zest'.
3 Heat the butter in a large frying pan and fry the liver in this with the heat fairly high, adding the grated orange rind and turning this in the butter at the same time you turn the liver.
4 Add the orange juice and seasoning, lower the heat and simmer gently until the meat is tender.
5 Dish up and garnish with rings of orange and chopped parsley.
6 Serve with fresh or frozen peas and canned or fresh new potatoes.

Shopping reminders:

Orange liver dish: lambs' or calves' liver, oranges, butter or margarine, seasoning, parsley, fresh or frozen peas (or use canned peas), fresh or canned new potatoes, mint.

Dessert: margarine, sugar, eggs, flour, jam or golden syrup.

Menu:
Prawn cocktail
Veal Cordon Bleu with green salad and new potatoes
Fresh fruit salad

Fresh fruit salad

Blend fresh fruit in season together, moisten with fresh orange juice, or for special occasions with Kirsch. Add a little sugar to taste, or combine some canned fruit with fresh fruit and use the syrup from the canned fruit to sweeten and moisten.

Prawn cocktail

no cooking

you will need for 4 servings:

4 oz. shelled fresh *or*
frozen prawns *or*
equivalent in canned
prawns
small portion lettuce

for the sauce:

3–4 tablespoons
mayonnaise
1 tablespoon tomato
ketchup
1 tablespoon thick
cream, optional

few drops Tabasco
sauce, optional
seasoning

to garnish:
1 lemon

1 If using frozen prawns allow to defrost at room temperature or in the refrigerator. Do not put into a hot place to defrost, as this rapid thawing toughens frozen shellfish.
2 Shred the lettuce very finely and put into 4 glasses or small dishes (remember it has to be eaten with a spoon, so make the pieces really tiny).
3 Blend the ingredients for the sauce and mix the prawns in this. Pile on the lettuce.
4 Arrange wedges of lemon at the side of the dish.

To vary:
a) **the sauce:** use sieved fresh tomato purée instead of tomato ketchup; add a few drops Worcestershire sauce; put in a little dry sherry to taste.
b) **the fish mixture:**
1 Use a mixture of shellfish and crab, with prawns and prepared mussels.
2 Blend shell and flaked white fish or flaked salmon.
3 Add tiny pieces of chopped green pepper, celery and gherkin or cucumber to the fish mixture.

Veal Cordon Bleu, with green salad and new potatoes

cooking time: 12 minutes

you will need for 4 servings:

4 thin fillets
(escalopes) of
veal
4 slices cheese*

4 slices cooked ham,
each half the size
of the veal

*Cheddar, Emmenthal, Gruyère, are all suitable

to coat:
½ oz. flour
seasoning
1 egg**
2 oz. crisp bread-
crumbs

to fry:
2 oz. butter
2 tablespoons olive
or frying oil

**or use 2 egg yolks and save the whites for an Alaska

1 Wash and dry the veal well.
2 Put the cheese and ham on one half of the veal, fold over to make a sandwich.
3 Mix flour and seasoning and dust veal lightly with this, then brush in beaten egg and coat with the crumbs, pressing these firmly against the meat.
4 Heat the butter and oil and fry the meat quickly on either side until golden brown, then lower the heat and cook gently for approximately 8 minutes until the meat is tender.
5 Drain on absorbent paper and serve with new potatoes (use canned for speed) and green salad.

To vary:
Fill with liver pâté instead of cheese and ham.

Green salad

A green salad should just consist of shredded lettuce, watercress, sliced green pepper and sliced cucumber. Chopped chicory can be added if wished.
Toss in a mixture of oil and lemon juice or vinegar, seasoned well (it is usual to blend twice as much oil as vinegar or lemon juice, and season with salt, pepper, mustard and a little sugar).
Chopped herbs may be added if wished.

Note: To save time, make large quantities of oil and vinegar (French dressing) and keep in a screw topped jar. Shake well before using.

Shopping reminders:
Prawn cocktail: prawns, lettuce, mayonnaise, tomato ketchup, thick cream, Tabasco sauce, seasoning, lemon.
Veal dish: veal, cheese, ham, flour, seasoning, egg, crisp breadcrumbs, butter, olive oil, lettuce, watercress, green pepper, cucumber, lemon, canned or fresh new potatoes, mint.
Dessert: canned and/or all fresh fruits in season, sugar, Kirsch (optional).

Menu:
Sardine salad
**Curried corned beef slices with rice or
   French bread and butter**
Cornflake crumble

Cornflake crumble

cooking time: few minutes

you will need for 4 servings:

3 oz. cornflakes	1½ oz. brown sugar
1½ oz. butter *or* margarine	large can apple sauce

1 Put the cornflakes into a bowl, then melt the butter, add to the cornflakes with the sugar and allow to cool.
2 Put half the mixture at the bottom of 4 dishes, top with the apple sauce then a final layer of cornflakes.

To vary:
Instead of cornflakes use coarse crumbs, heat 2 oz. butter then toss in the crumbs until golden brown, then add the brown sugar.
Use another fruit purée instead of apple.
Add dried fruit to the apple purée.

Curried corned beef slices with rice or French bread and butter

cooking time: 15 minutes

you will need for 4 servings:

1 onion	1 teaspoon sugar
1 small apple	12 oz. – 1 lb.
2 oz. fat	corned beef
1–2 teaspoons curry powder	
2 teaspoons flour	**to serve:**
½ pint brown stock *or* water and one beef stock cube	1–2 oz. desiccated coconut
seasoning	chutney
	1–2 bananas

1 Peel and grate both the onion and the apple.
2 Heat the fat in a large frying pan and fry the onion and apple for a few minutes. Add the curry powder, flour, and stir well into the onion mixture, then blend in the liquid, bring to the boil and cook until slightly thickened.
3 Add the seasoning and sugar.

4 Cut the corned beef into neat slices and heat in the sauce.
5 Dish up and serve sprinkled lightly with coconut; accompany with chutney and sliced bananas.
Note: You can serve this with boiled rice as is normal with a curry, or it is very good with crusty French bread and butter.

To vary:
Curried ham: heat thick slices of boiled bacon or cooked ham in the curry sauce. Since dried fruit blends well with ham, add 1–2 oz. sultanas to the curry sauce.
Curried tongue: heat thick slices of cooked tongue in the sauce. Tongue is improved by a slightly sweeter flavoured sauce, so either increase the amount of sugar or blend a tablespoon of chutney into the sauce.
Curried luncheon meat: cut canned luncheon meat into slices and heat in the curry sauce. The sauce is improved if ½ tablespoon of concentrated tomato purée or 1–2 skinned chopped tomatoes are fried with the onion and apple.

Sardine salad

Open a can of sardines in oil or tomato sauce and arrange on a bed of lettuce. Garnish with sliced tomato, cucumber and other salad ingredients.

Shopping reminders:
Sardine salad: sardines, lettuce, tomatoes, cucumber and other salad ingredients.
Corned beef dish: onion, apple, fat, curry powder, flour, stock cube (if no stock available), seasoning, sugar, corned beef, desiccated coconut, chutney, bananas, rice or French bread, butter.
Dessert: cornflakes, butter or margarine, brown sugar, can apple sauce.

Menu:
Avocado pears vinaigrette
**Fried chicken with corn, fried
   bananas and broccoli**
Pears with raspberry cream

Fried chicken with corn, fried bananas and broccoli

cooking time: 15-20 minutes

you will need for 4 servings:

4 joints young frying
   chicken

to coat:

1 oz. flour
seasoning
1 egg
2 oz. crisp bread-
   crumbs

to fry:

2 oz. butter
2 tablespoons olive
   or frying oil

to serve:

canned corn
2 bananas
broccoli

1 If using frozen chicken allow to defrost before cooking.

2 Blend the flour with seasoning and coat the well-dried chicken in this.

3 Brush with beaten egg and roll in the crumbs.

4 Heat the butter and oil together in a large pan and fry the chicken steadily, turning over several times, until crisp and golden brown and tender.

5 Lift from the pan and keep hot.

6 Meanwhile heat the corn; halve and fry the bananas in the fat remaining in the pan.

7 Arrange round the joints of chicken.

8 Cook and serve the broccoli separately.

6 simple ways to vary fried chicken

Herb coated chicken

Coat the chicken with beaten egg and parsley and thyme packet stuffing; add a little extra freshly chopped herbs if wished.

Sausagemeat coating

Blend 8 oz. sausagemeat with 1 egg yolk, and 1 tablespoon chopped parsley. Press this round the joints of chicken to give a thin coating. Dip in egg white and crumbs and fry as basic recipe.

Deep fried chicken

Coat the chicken as above and fry in deep hot oil or fat until tender. Young chicken joints will probably take only 12–15 minutes.

Hasty fried chicken

Buy ready-cooked chicken and just warm through in the butter and oil. Garnish with sliced green and red peppers. Serve with canned Bolognese or barbecue sauce, or use recipe on page 80.

Cheese fried chicken

Blend 1–2 oz. grated Parmesan cheese with the breadcrumbs – do not overcook this version.

Curried fried chicken

Blend curry powder with the flour in coating the chicken and again with the breadcrumbs or beaten egg to ensure a fairly strong flavour.

More elaborate ways of using frying chicken

Speedy coq au vin

Coat the chicken in seasoned flour only. Fry as the basic recipe until just brown, then add about $\frac{1}{2}$ pint cheap white or red wine, or $\frac{1}{4}$ pint wine and $\frac{1}{4}$ pint stock, together with 2–4 oz. small mushrooms and about 2 tablespoons cocktail onions. Continue cooking for a further 15 minutes, then serve with creamed potatoes or boiled rice.

Speedy chicken Portuguese

Coat the joints of chicken in seasoned flour and fry as basic recipe, lift out of pan. Fry 1–2 finely chopped or grated onions in any fat remaining in the pan, then add either a medium sized can of tomatoes plus the liquid (or a medium can concentrated tomato soup), flavour with celery salt and garlic salt, place the joints of chicken in this and cook until very tender. Serve with boiled rice or creamed potatoes.

Chicken in cream

Coat the chicken with seasoned flour only. Fry in the butter (omit olive oil) for a few minutes until pale golden colour, then lower the heat and add about 4 tablespoons chicken stock, or water with about $\frac{1}{4}$ of a chicken stock cube. Simmer steadily for approximately 10 minutes, making sure the liquid does not entirely evaporate. Stir in $\frac{1}{4}$ pint thin cream and 2 table-spoons sherry. Season well and heat gently for a few minutes before serving with rice, or new or creamed potatoes, and peas or a green vegetable.

Curried creamed chicken

Coat the joints of chicken in flour, to which seasoning, a little dry mustard and curry powder have been added. Fry in 2–3 oz. hot butter until just tender, then add $\frac{1}{4}$ pint thin cream, blended with a little more curry powder, heat gently. Serve with boiled rice and chutney.

A sprinkling of coconut may be added to the chicken *WITH* the cream.

Grilled chicken
Brush the joints of chicken with melted butter and grill quickly until brown and crisp, then lower the heat and/or move the grill pan further away from the heat and continue cooking until quite tender.

Lemon grilled chicken
Blend finely grated lemon rind with the butter and baste the chicken with seasoned lemon juice during cooking.

Grilled devilled chicken
Blend curry powder and chutney with the butter, together with a few drops Worcestershire sauce. Baste the chicken with this during cooking.

Paprika chicken
Blend 1–2 teaspoons paprika pepper with the butter used in basting the chicken during grilling.

Pears with raspberry cream
Whip ¼ pint thick cream until it just holds its shape, then blend with 4–6 oz. fresh raspberries and sugar to taste, or with well-drained frozen raspberries and sugar. Pile into 4 large or 8 small pear halves and chill. Serve with wafer biscuits.

Avocado pears vinaigrette
Halve ripe avocado pears (you can tell if ripe by the way the flesh 'yields' when pressed very gently with your finger tip at the stalk end). Remove the stone and fill each half with dressing made by blending seasoning, a pinch of dry mustard, pinch sugar, 3 tablespoons olive oil and 1½ tablespoons lemon juice or vinegar. Serve with a teaspoon.

To vary:
Fill the halved avocado pears with prawns or other shellfish in mayonnaise.
Blend a little curry powder with the mayonnaise and shellfish (generally called **Avocado Egyptienne**).

Avocado Mexicaine: halve 2 pears carefully – do not damage skin. Remove the ripe flesh from the halved avocado pears. Blend with a few drops Tabasco sauce, 1 teaspoon olive oil, 1 tablespoon lemon juice, seasoning. Mash until smooth, then pile back into the 4 halves of the avocado pears and serve.

Shopping reminders:
Avocado pears: avocado pears, salt, pepper, mustard, sugar, oil, lemon juice or vinegar.
Fried chicken, etc.: jointed chicken, flour, salt, pepper, egg, crumbs, butter, oil, canned corn, bananas, broccoli.
Dessert: medium to large can pears, thick cream, fresh or frozen raspberries, sugar, wafer biscuits.

Meals that take no more than 1½ hours to cook

In this section are menus where no dish or combination of dishes take more than 1½ hours to cook. The dishes are not difficult or time-consuming to prepare; often they can be got ready and left to cook while you carry on with other jobs or sit and relax.

In many cases part of the dish (e.g. the stuffing for hearts on page 58; the 'blanching' and simmering of sweetbreads, page 59 etc.) could be done earlier, so shortening the cooking time when you come home tired.

Because of the various *methods* of cooking, i.e. frying, etc. and the fact that the *complete menu* does not take the same cooking time, it is not suggested that these particular menus, as they are given, are suitable for automatic cooking, but often you could adapt them for an automatic cooker if you wished.

In this, as in the previous chapter, the menu is given in the order of serving, but the recipes are given in the order of cooking.

Menu:
Shellfish salads
Cheese and vegetable Yorkshire
   pudding with baked tomatoes
Chocolate apricot pudding

Chocolate apricot pudding [F]

cooking time: 1½ hours

you will need for 4 servings:
for the sponge:

3 oz. quick creaming margarine	4 oz. self-raising flour
3 oz. castor sugar	2 oz. chocolate powder
2 large eggs	

for base of pudding: small can apricots

1 Put all the ingredients for the sponge into a large bowl and cream until smooth.
2 Drain the apricots and put at the bottom of a greased 2–pint basin, cover with the chocolate sponge mixture.
3 Cover the pudding with well-greased grease-proof paper or foil.
4 Steam for 1¼–1½ hours, turn out and serve with the hot syrup from the can, or this can be made into a lemon apricot sauce, see below.

To vary:

Lemon apricot pudding: omit the chocolate powder and use 5 oz. flour and add finely grated rind of 2 lemons to the other sponge ingredients. Serve with lemon apricot sauce, see below.

Jam sponge pudding: put jam at the base of the pudding basin and top with the chocolate mixture or a plain vanilla sponge made by creaming 3 oz. margarine, 4 oz. sugar, 2 large eggs and 5 oz. self-raising flour with 1 tablespoon milk. Serve with jam sauce.

Syrup sponge pudding: as jam sponge pudding, but serve with lemon syrup sauce.

When in a hurry!

Remember there are very good canned or prepared sponge puddings that just need heating through and can be served with quick sauces.

Some easy sauces to serve with sponge puddings

Lemon apricot sauce

Blend ½ pint syrup from a can of apricots with 2 teaspoons arrowroot or cornflour, 2 oz. sugar and the juice of 1 large lemon. Heat until a clear thickened sauce, stir well. If you have not enough apricot syrup, add sufficient water to give ½ pint and 1–2 tablespoons apricot jam to give extra flavour.

Jam sauce

Put ¼ lb. jam, ¼ pint water, blended with 2 teaspoons arrowroot or cornflour with a little lemon juice to give a 'bite'. Heat, stir well until smooth and thickened.

Lemon syrup sauce

Put ¼ lb. golden syrup, grated rind of 1 lemon, 3 tablespoons lemon juice and 4 tablespoons water in a saucepan, heat until well blended.

Cheese and vegetable Yorkshire pudding with baked tomatoes

cooking time: approximately 35–40 minutes

you will need for 4 servings:

1 oz. fat	pinch salt
8–12 oz. cooked vegetables	1 egg
	½ pint milk, *or use* ⅔ milk, ⅓ water
for the batter:	4 oz. grated Cheddar cheese
4 oz. flour, preferably plain	

1 Heat the fat in an ovenproof serving dish or a Yorkshire pudding tin.
2 Toss the vegetables in this, then top with the cheese-flavoured batter, made by blending all the ingredients together.
3 Bake towards the top of a hot oven (425–450°F., Gas Mark 6–7) until crisp and golden brown, lower heat if necessary.
4 Serve at once, either with baked tomatoes or a tomato sauce, see pages 79, 81.

To vary:

Toad-in-the-hole. Heat approximately 1 lb. sausages in the fat for 5–10 minutes (depending on the size). Omit the cheese from the batter, pour this over the sausages and cook as above.

Lamb toad-in-the-hole

Heat 4 lamb chops in the fat and continue as above.

Mixed toad-in-the-hole

Heat fingers of steak, halved kidneys, halved

tomatoes and small sausages in the fat and continue as above.

Mushroom toad-in-the-hole

Toss approximately 4–6 oz. mushrooms in the fat, do not pre-cook, add the plain or cheese-flavoured batter and cook as above.

Sweet batters

These are extremely good for a quick pudding.

Norfolk pudding

Heat 2 good-sized peeled and sliced cooking apples and 1–2 oz. sultanas or raisins in the fat for about 5 minutes. Sprinkle with sugar, then add the batter and cook as above.

Plum and almond batter

Heat halved fresh plums and 1 oz. blanched almonds in the fat for approximately 5 minutes. Cover with the batter and cook as above.

Shellfish salads

Blend 4 tablespoons mayonnaise with 1 tablespoon tomato ketchup. Toss 4–6 oz. shelled prawns or other shellfish in this. Arrange on small plates, garnished with lettuce, cucumber and lemon slices.

Shopping reminders:
Shellfish salads: mayonnaise, tomato ketchup, prawns, lettuce, cucumber, lemon.
Cheese and vegetable Yorkshire pudding: fat, vegetables, flour, salt, egg, milk, Cheddar cheese, tomatoes.
Dessert: margarine, sugar, eggs, self-raising flour, chocolate powder, apricots.

Menu:
**American fish pie and
   green vegetable (spinach)
Burgundy pears
Cheese and biscuits**

Burgundy pears

cooking time: 5 minutes

you will need for 6 servings:

large can pear halves	few drops cochineal
½ pint Burgundy	½ oz. powdered gelatine

to decorate:
¼ pint thick cream
4–6 glacé cherries

1 Drain the pears from the syrup. Measure the syrup and if less than ½ pint add either water or a little extra wine.
2 Reserve two pear halves for decoration, and put the remainder with the ½ pint of wine and 2 or 3 drops of cochineal into a pan.
3 Bring to the boil, then reduce the heat and simmer for 5 minutes only.
4 Meanwhile dissolve the gelatine in the measured pear syrup.
5 Lift the pears from the pan – they should now be a very delicate pale pink – and put them into a shallow dish.
6 Add the wine liquid to the pear syrup and gelatine – when cool, pour over the pears.
7 Allow to set, then decorate with the remaining two pear halves (cut into thin slices and arranged to form a flower design) the cream, and the glacé cherries.

To vary:
Use ripe dessert pears instead of canned pears, dilute the wine with ½ pint water and sweeten with 2–3 oz. sugar.

American fish pie [F] and green vegetable

cooking time: 45 minutes

you will need for 4 servings:

1¼ lb. white fish (weight without bone or skin)	1 oz. flour
	8 oz. tomatoes
	4 tablespoons water
seasoning	6 oz. flaky pastry
2 onions	(see page 74)
2 rashers bacon	*or* use 8–9 oz.
2 oz. butter	frozen puff pastry

to glaze:

1 egg	1 tablespoon water

to garnish:

parsley	1 lemon

1 Simmer fish in water to cover with seasoning until just tender but slightly undercooked.
2 Save ½ pint liquid and cut fish into neat pieces.
3 Chop onions and bacon finely.

4 Fry in hot butter until the onions are really tender. Lift on to a plate.
5 Stir the flour into any fat remaining in the pan, cook for 2 or 3 minutes, then gradually add the skinned and chopped tomatoes with the water and fish stock.
6 Bring to the boil and cook until a smooth sauce.
7 Add the fish, bacon and onions. Put into a pie dish and cover with pastry.
8 Beat the egg and water, brush over the pastry and bake the pie for approximately 25–30 minutes in the centre of a hot oven (425–450°F., Gas Mark 6–7).*
9 Arrange the garnish round the pie. Serve hot with green vegetable or salad.
*Turn heat down if the pastry is becoming too brown before the filling is cooked.

To vary:
Omit the bacon, and add 2 oz. chopped mushrooms to the onions.
Add 1 teaspoon curry powder to the onions at stage 3, to make curried fish pie.
Top with creamed potatoes instead of pastry; bake for 25 minutes only.

Shopping reminders:
American fish pie: white fish, salt, pepper, onions, bacon, butter, egg, flour, tomatoes, frozen puff pastry (or ingredients for flaky pastry), parsley, lemon, spinach or salad.
Burgundy pears: canned pears, Burgundy, cochineal, powdered gelatine, thick cream, glacé cherries.
Cheese and biscuits: cheese, biscuits, butter, celery and/or watercress.

Menu:
Onion consommé
Bacon and egg pie, jacket potatoes, peas
Orange and apple salad

Jacket potatoes

Choose a medium to large sized potato per person. Wash and dry the potatoes. Prick with a fork or fine skewer so that the potatoes do not 'burst' in cooking. The ideal temperature at which to cook jacket potatoes is in a moderate oven (350–375°F., Gas Mark 4–5) and a medium potato takes an hour at this temperature. If you use a lower temperature, adjust the time accordingly. Where you have a period when the oven heat is raised, as in this menu, it is a good idea to move the potatoes to the coolest part of the oven for a time. When cooked, split the potatoes with a knife or mark with a cross and top with butter.

To vary:
[F] **Cheesy potatoes:** bake potatoes until soft. Halve (take care as you handle them as they are very hot). Spoon the pulp into a basin – keep the cases intact. Add seasoning, a little butter or margarine and grated cheese to taste. Pile back into the potato cases and reheat for about 10 minutes. These can be prepared earlier and reheated for about 25–30 minutes.
[F] **Ham potatoes:** add finely chopped cooked ham instead of grated cheese.

Bacon and egg pie, with peas

cooking time: 40 minutes

you will need for 4–5 servings:

for the pastry:	for the filling:
10–12 oz. flour preferably plain*	12 oz. bacon (streaky *or* back)
pinch salt	4–5 eggs
5–6 oz. fat*	pepper
water to mix	
	to glaze:
	1 egg

*depending on thickness of pastry, or buy 1 lb. frozen short crust pastry.

1 Make pastry as short crust, page 73.
2 Roll out half the pastry and line an 8-inch pie plate.
3 Chop the bacon rashers finely, put over the pastry (if you like crisp bacon these pieces should be fried for a few minutes).
4 Crack the eggs into a basin, then pour them over the bacon. Season with pepper.
5 Roll out the remaining pastry, cover the eggs, etc., seal the edges, flute these, then use any pieces of pastry left to make decorative shapes, such as leaves or a tassel.
6 Put these on top of the pastry, moistening them so they 'stick' firmly.
7 Brush with beaten egg.
8 Bake in the centre of a hot oven (425–450°F.,

Gas Mark 6–7) for 15–20 minutes to set the pastry, then lower the heat to moderate for a further 20–25 minutes. Serve with peas.

To vary:

Note: Although one of the variations is marked [F] to denote it freezes well, the other recipes do not, as the eggs become very hard and tough.

Meat and egg pie: blend minced cooked meat, or flaked corned beef or canned stewing steak with a little grated onion and skinned chopped tomatoes, season. Use in place of the bacon, top with eggs and proceed as above.

Chicken and egg pie: chop cooked chicken or mix chicken and bacon. Moisten with a little thin cream, season well, top with eggs and bake.

[F] **Meat and vegetable pie:** cover the pastry with cooked or canned steak, then a layer of thickly sliced tomatoes, grated onion and sliced fried mushrooms. Top with pastry and bake as bacon and egg pie.

Orange and apple salad

Cut away the peel from 4 oranges and 4 dessert apples (core these). Slice thinly, arrange in layers in sundae glasses and serve with thin cream.

Onion consommé

Grate 2 medium sized onions and toss in 1 oz. butter in a pan until just tender. Add 2 cans of consommé and heat. Just before serving, top with a little grated Parmesan cheese.

Shopping reminders:

Soup: onions, butter, canned consommé.
Bacon and egg pie, etc.: either flour, salt and fat for pastry or frozen short crust pastry, bacon, eggs, pepper, potatoes, butter, peas.
Dessert: oranges, apples, thin cream.

Menu:
Smoked trout and horseradish cream
**Bacon and bean bake with cauliflower
   and scalloped potatoes**
Fruit slices

Scalloped potatoes

cooking time: 1–1¼ hours

you will need for 4 servings:

1 lb. old *or* new potatoes (weight when peeled or scraped) seasoning	2 oz. butter ½ pint milk

1 Cut the potatoes into wafer-thin slices and put into a pie dish or ovenproof dish, seasoning each layer well.
2 Heat the butter and milk together then pour over the potatoes.
3 Bake in the coolest part of the oven. Normally they can be baked for approximately 1¼ hours in a moderate oven or 1½ hours in a very moderate oven. However, in this particular menu where the heat is raised to moderately hot for a period they will take between 1–1¼ hours.

To vary:

Scalloped potatoes Provençal: rub the dish with a cut clove of garlic, then sandwich each layer of potatoes with wafer-thin slices of onion and skinned tomato. Brush with melted butter or margarine, season well, but omit the milk.

Savoury scalloped potatoes: use canned mushroom or cream of chicken soup instead of milk.

Cheese scalloped potatoes: sprinkle each layer of potatoes with grated Cheddar or Gruyère cheese – do not use too much.

Fruit slices

Make the fleur pastry as instructed on page 73, and roll out into a neat oblong shape. Prick, and bake on a baking sheet for approximately 25 minutes towards the top of a moderately hot oven (375–400°F., Gas Mark 5–6) until golden brown. Allow to cool, then top with sliced ice cream and fresh or well-drained canned fruit just before serving. Cut into slices to serve.

Note: pastry made with 6 oz. flour gives 4 very generous portions, or 6 smaller ones.

Bacon and bean bake with cauliflower

cooking time: 30 minutes

you will need for 4 servings:

8 oz. streaky or
    back bacon
1 medium can baked
    beans in tomato
    sauce
2–3 hard-boiled
    eggs
¼ pint tomato juice
    or stock

for the topping:

2 oz. margarine
2 oz. soft bread-
    crumbs

to garnish:

1–2 sliced tomatoes

1 Cut the bacon into small pieces and fry until crisp and golden brown.

2 Then put into a pie dish with the beans, the hard-boiled eggs and the liquid.

3 Add the margarine to any bacon fat remaining in the frying pan, toss the crumbs in this for a few minutes only and press over the top of the bean mixture.

4 Bake for 20–25 minutes towards the top of a moderately hot oven (375–400°F., Gas Mark 5–6). Garnish with sliced tomatoes.

To vary:
Use canned sweetcorn in place of baked beans, with tomato juice (not stock) as the liquid.
Add mixed cooked vegetables in place of baked beans. Again, these are nicer if blended with tomato juice rather than stock.

Smoked trout

You buy these all ready to serve. Put one on each plate, garnished with a good thick wedge of lemon and one or two lettuce leaves. Serve with horseradish cream and thin brown bread and butter.

Shopping reminders:

Trout: smoked trout, lemon, lettuce, horseradish cream, brown bread, butter.
Bacon and bean bake, etc.: bacon, canned beans in tomato sauce, eggs, tomato juice, margarine, bread, tomatoes, cauliflower, salt, pepper, potatoes, butter, milk.
Dessert: flour, butter, sugar, egg for the fleur

pastry (or buy frozen short crust pastry instead), ice cream, fresh or canned fruit.

Menu:
Canned asparagus soup
Bacon olives
    with oven fried potatoes and
    sprouts or cabbage
Quick apple crumble

Bacon olives with oven fried potatoes, and sprouts or cabbage

cooking time: 35–45 minutes

you will need for 4 servings:

4 thin slices
    middle gammon
packet sage and
    onion stuffing, or
    home-made
    stuffing, page 71

2 bottles tomato
    juice or 1 pint
    can

to garnish:
can sweetcorn

to serve:
oven fried potatoes
    (see below)

sprouts or
    cabbage

1 Cut the rinds from the gammon rashers and lay them flat on a board.

2 Make up the stuffing as directed on the packet or in the recipe, but keep it sufficiently stiff to form into 4 finger-shapes.

3 Put one on each gammon slice and roll firmly, then tie with cotton, or use a skewer to fasten.

4 Put into a casserole, pour over the tomato juice, cover with a lid or foil.

5 Bake for 35–45 minutes in the centre of a very moderate to moderate oven (350–375°F., Gas Mark 3–4).

6 Lift on to a dish, cover with a little of the tomato liquid and arrange the heated sweetcorn around the dish. Serve the rest of the tomato liquid separately.

Oven fried potatoes

Peel old potatoes and cut into thick slices. Brush a large flat baking tray with melted fat, arrange the potatoes on this, then brush with more fat. Cook in the hottest part of the oven for approximately 35–40 minutes, until crisp and golden brown.

Quick apple crumble

cooking time: 25–30 minutes

you will need for 4 servings:

1 can apple pie filling	grated rind and juice of 1 lemon

for the crumble:

2 oz. margarine	3 oz. castor sugar
4 oz. plain or self-raising flour	grated rind of 1 lemon

1 Tip the apple pie filling into a 1½–2-pint pie dish.

2 Add the lemon juice and rind and stir together.

3 Rub the margarine into the flour, add the sugar and the grated lemon rind.

4 Press on top of the apple mixture and bake in the centre of a very moderate to moderate oven (350–375°F., Gas Mark 3–4) for approximately 25–30 minutes.

5 Serve hot.

Shopping reminders:

Canned soup: asparagus.
Bacon olives: gammon, tomato juice, sage and onion stuffing, can sweetcorn, potatoes, sprouts or cabbage.
Apple crumble: apple pie filling, lemons, margarine, flour, sugar.

Menu:
Tomato juice cocktail
Stuffed lambs' hearts, creamed potatoes, green vegetable
Fruit amber

Stuffed lambs' hearts, [F] creamed potatoes, green vegetable

cooking time: 1¼–1½ hours

you will need for 4 servings:

4 medium sized lambs' hearts	2 oz. butter or margarine
seasoning	stuffing,* see below

*Any stuffing would be suitable, but sage and onion or herb stuffing, are excellent, see pages 70 and 71.

1 If you buy frozen hearts allow these to defrost before cooking.

2 Soak the hearts in cold water, to which you add a little salt, for about 10 minutes, minimum, to draw out the blood.

3 Cut the base of the hearts so that you can remove the arteries. If you find this difficult then cut the hearts in two – they can easily be tied or skewered together.

4 Make the stuffing; fill each well-dried, seasoned heart with this.

5 If using foil (which means longer cooking but a very moist outside to the hearts) spread 4 squares of foil with the butter or margarine. Lay one heart on each piece of foil and wrap firmly.

6 If you do not use foil you will have a crisp outside to the hearts. In this case you should spread the butter round hearts, to encourage browning and keep them moist.

7 Put the foil-wrapped or greased hearts into the roasting tin.

8 Cook for 1¼ hours or 1½ hours towards the top of a very moderate oven (325–350°F., Gas Mark 3–4). You will need the longer cooking time when wrapping the meat: naturally if you buy larger hearts the cooking time will be even longer.

9 Serve the hearts either with the meat juice that runs into each foil package or with thickened gravy, see page 78, and accompany with creamed potatoes and green vegetable.

Fruit amber

cooking time: 55 minutes

you will need for 4 servings:

1 pint very thick sweetened fruit purée, or equivalent in fruit pie filling	2 eggs
	2 oz. sugar

1 Have the fruit purée ready in a basin. Separate the eggs and beat the yolks into the fruit.

2 Put into pie dish and set for 30 minutes in the centre of a very moderate oven (325–350°F., Gas Mark 3–4).

3 Whisk the egg whites until stiff, add the sugar (as page 68).

4 Pile over fruit mixture then return to the oven and set for 25 minutes. Serve hot.

Note: If serving cold use 4 oz. sugar and set for at least 1 hour, as for meringues, page 68.

To vary:

Crumble amber: add 2 oz. crisped breadcrumbs to the fruit at stage 1.

Coconut amber: add 2 oz. desiccated coconut to the fruit at stage 1, and 1–2 oz. desiccated coconut to the meringue at stage 3, after adding the sugar.

Tomato juice cocktail

Open 1 large can of tomato juice, or the equivalent in bottled tomato juice. Flavour with celery salt, a pinch of cayenne pepper, and a little Worcestershire sauce. In summer this is improved if several sprigs of mint and a few ice cubes are put into the tomato juice and it is allowed to stand in a cool place for an hour.

A little dry sherry can also be mixed with the tomato juice.

Shopping reminders:

Tomato juice cocktail: canned or bottled tomato juice, celery salt, cayenne pepper, Worcestershire sauce and/or sherry, mint, (optional).

Stuffed hearts, etc.: lambs' hearts, ingredients for selected stuffing, butter or margarine, seasoning, potatoes and a little milk for creaming, green vegetable, ingredients for gravy, see page 78.

Fruit amber: either canned fruit, pie filling or fruit in season, eggs, sugar.

Menu:
Pâté with toast and butter
Fried sweetbreads with tomato and mushroom purée, watercress salad
Sweet omelette

Fried sweetbreads with tomato and mushroom purée

cooking time: 40 minutes

you will need for 4 servings:

minimum of 1 lb. lambs' *or* calves' sweetbreads*	seasoning

to coat:
1 egg
2 oz. crisp breadcrumbs

for the purée:
large can tomatoes
pinch curry powder
pinch mixed herbs

to fry:
3–4 oz. fat

to garnish:
1 lemon

seasoning
2–4 oz. mushrooms

*It is often difficult to buy fresh sweetbreads today, but the frozen ones are excellent. It does mean, however, that you need to be fairly generous with the quantity of frozen sweetbreads which you buy, since they seem to 'shrink' drastically when cooked.

1 First 'blanch' either fresh or frozen sweetbreads; this means putting them into cold water, then bringing the water to the boil in the case of fresh meat; or allowing the sweetbreads to simmer gently until defrosted in the case of frozen meat. The purpose of 'blanching' is to whiten the sweetbreads.

2 Throw away the water, then put the 'blanched' sweetbreads into fresh cold water, season well and bring the water to the boil.

3 Remove any grey 'scum' that may come to the top of the water, lower the heat and simmer for approximately 25 minutes until just tender.

4 When you have time you can cool the sweetbreads and remove all the very thin skins, but when time is short, drain them, dry on kitchen paper, and coat in the egg and crumbs while they are still warm. The easiest method of doing this is to put the beaten egg into a bowl and turn the sweetbreads in this. Then put the crumbs into a large paper bag, drop the egg-coated sweetbreads into this, and shake firmly until they are evenly coated.

5 Fry in the hot fat until crisp and brown, and drain on absorbent paper.

6 Garnish with lemon and serve with the tomato and mushroom purée, which is made by simmering the tomatoes with the other ingredients – the mushrooms should be cut into thin slices before cooking with the tomatoes.

Some other ways to cook sweetbreads

Creamed sweetbreads

Blanch the sweetbreads as stage 1 in the recipe above, then simmer as stages 2 and 3. Meanwhile make a sauce with 1 oz. butter, 1 oz. flour, ½ pint milk, seasoning and ¼ pint thin cream. Put the skinned sweetbreads into this and simmer gently for approximately 10–15 minutes. If the sauce is becoming too thick then dilute with either a little more milk or chicken stock. Sliced mushrooms may be added to the sauce. Garnish with canned asparagus tips.

Sweetbreads in savoury tomato sauce

Make the tomato purée as recipe above. Blend ½ oz. cornflour with 4 tablespoons chicken stock or water, add to the tomato purée and cook until slightly thickened. Stir in 1 oz. butter or margarine and 1 grated or finely chopped onion (or equivalent in dehydrated onion). Blanch the sweetbreads as recipe above. Put into the tomato sauce and simmer gently for 30 minutes. If preferred cook as stages 2 and 3, so that you can remove the skins, then simmer in the tomato mixture for approximately 10–15 minutes.

Oven 'fried' sweetbreads

Frying food is a troublesome method, when you are busy, for it means you must watch the food as it cooks. If more convenient the sweetbreads may be crisped in the oven: 'blanch' and simmer as stages 1–3 above, and coat as given in the basic recipe. Grease and heat a baking tray well (this prevents the sweetbreads sticking to the tin). Sprinkle a little oil over the coated sweetbreads (being careful not to disturb the crumbs). Cook for 15 minutes towards the top of a moderately hot oven until crisp, brown and very hot.

Watercress salad

Buy a good quantity of watercress, remove the leaves and toss them in well-seasoned oil and vinegar.

Pâté

An easy recipe for home-made pâté is given on page 63, but excellent pâté may be purchased. Cut into neat portions (allow 1–1½ oz. per person), put on the plate and garnish either with lettuce or lemon slices. Serve with hot toast and with butter.

Sweet omelette

This is not a usual dessert in this country but it is a very delicious one. It must be cooked at the last minute, but all preparations *can* be made beforehand, including whisking up the egg whites, see method, stage 3.

cooking time: few minutes

you will need for 4 servings:

4–6 eggs	2 tablespoons cream from the top of the milk *or* thin cream
1 oz. sugar	1 oz. butter

for the filling:	to decorate:
about 3–4 table-spoons jam *or* fruit purée (canned fruit pie fillings *or* canned chopped fruit are excellent)	1–2 tablespoons sieved icing sugar

1 Separate the egg whites and the yolks.
2 Beat the yolks with the sugar and milk.
3 Whisk the egg whites until very stiff.
  If you want to prepare the whites beforehand: *if you choose a bowl with a perfectly flat rim in which to whisk the egg whites you can turn the bowl upside down over a flat plate and you will find the whites will stay stiff for about 30 minutes* OR if preferred cover the top of the bowl with foil and seal tightly. Should the air come into contact with the egg whites they will become liquid again, and need another whisk before the next stage.
4 Fold the stiffly beaten egg whites into the egg yolks with a metal spoon.
5 Heat the butter in a good sized omelette pan, and meanwhile heat the grill and warm the jam or fruit purée.
6 Pour the egg mixture into the hot butter and cook until just set on the bottom side.
7 Next put the omelette pan under the grill – make sure the handle is not likely to scorch.
8 Heat under the grill until the top of the omelette is just set, fill with the hot jam or fruit, fold over and tip on to a hot dish. Top with a dusting of icing sugar.

Other fillings for sweet omelettes:

Ice cream; macaroon biscuits – crumbled and

soaked in sherry; heated redcurrant jelly or marmalade.

Shopping reminders:

Pâté: either ingredients for home-made pâté, see page 63 or bought pâté, bread, butter, lemon or lettuce to garnish.

Fried sweetbreads, etc.: sweetbreads, seasoning, egg, crisp breadcrumbs, fat, lemon, canned tomatoes, curry powder, mixed herbs, mushrooms, watercress, oil, vinegar.

Sweet omelette: eggs, sugar, cream or milk, butter, jam or fruit, icing sugar.

Menu:
Grapefruit
Casserole of liver and beans with jacket potatoes and sprouts
Queen of puddings

Casserole of liver and beans [F] with jacket potatoes and sprouts

cooking time: 1½ hours

you will need for 4 servings:

12 oz.–1 lb. lambs' or calves' liver	½ pint brown stock *or* water and 1 beef stock cube
4 oz. streaky bacon	medium can baked beans
2 onions	small can tomatoes
2 oz. fat	seasoning
1 oz. flour	pinch sugar, optional

1 Cut the liver into neat pieces, remove the rinds from the bacon and dice.
2 Peel and chop the onions.
3 Heat the fat in a pan, toss the liver and bacon in this for a few minutes, put into a casserole.
4 Turn the onions in the fat until transparent, do not allow to brown, add to the meat in the casserole.
5 Blend the flour with any fat remaining in the pan, then gradually add the stock, bring to the boil and cook until thickened. Add the rest of the ingredients, seasoning well. A pinch of sugar may be added if wished, as this takes away the 'bite' from the liver.

6 Pour over the liver and bacon, cover the casserole and cook for 1–1¼ hours in the centre of a very moderate oven (325–350°F., Gas Mark 3–4).

The jacket potatoes should be put in at much the same time. Serve with sprouts.

To vary:
Thickly sliced ox-liver could be used, but the cooking time should be lengthened to 2¼ hours. Mushrooms or sliced carrots may be used instead of beans.

Omit the tomatoes and add ¾ pint stock.

Some other ways of cooking liver

Liver is a highly nutritious food, it provides iron as well as protein, so is important in the family diet.

Fried liver and bacon

Coat the sliced lambs' or calves' liver with seasoned flour – do not coat too thickly, otherwise you have a very hard outside to the liver. Fry in hot fat or butter until just tender. Do not over-cook for this toughens the meat. When cooked keep hot and fry the rashers of bacon in the pan. Serve with grilled or fried tomatoes.

The residue left in the frying pan is excellent for the basis of a good gravy.

Note: a little sugar added to the seasoning helps to counteract the 'bite' of liver which some people dislike.

Liver in soured cream and mushrooms

First, fry the mushrooms in the pan, lift out and keep hot. Add additional fat and then fry the coated slices of liver. When cooked remove the meat to a hot dish with the mushrooms.

To serve 4 people add ¼ pint dairy soured cream (or ¼ pint thin cream with 1 tablespoon lemon juice) to the meat juices remaining in the pan. Stir over a VERY LOW HEAT and season well.

See also Orange liver slices, page 48.

Oven baked liver

Put wafer-thin slices of well seasoned onion

61

and thicker slices of well seasoned tomato into a greased dish. Top with thin slices of seasoned liver, then more slices of onion and a final layer of tomato and a little butter. Cover the dish and bake for approximately 45 minutes–1 hour in the centre of a moderate oven (350–375°F., Gas Mark 4–5).

Queen of puddings

cooking time: 1 hour 5–10 minutes

you will need for 4 servings:

2 oz. cake *or* bread- crumbs	¾ pint milk 3–4 tablespoons
2 eggs	jam *or* fruit
3 oz. sugar*	purée

1 Put crumbs into basin, with egg yolks and 1 oz. of the sugar.
2 Beat well and add the warmed milk.
3 Spread half the jam or purée over base of a 1½–2 pint pie dish and put in the crumb mixture. Set for approximately 45 minutes in the centre of a very moderate oven (325–350°F., Gas Mark 3–4).
4 Whisk the egg whites stiffly, add sugar (as page 68).

5 Spread pudding with rest of jam or purée, then pile over the meringue and return to the oven for further 20–25 minutes. Serve hot.

Note: If serving cold you need 4 oz. sugar for the meringue topping, and to allow to set for at least 1 hour, as for meringues, see page 68.

To vary:
Chocolate Queen of puddings: either use crumbs of chocolate cake or add 1–2 oz. chocolate powder to egg yolks at Stage 1.

Swiss roll pudding: put 4 slices Swiss roll into pie dish then cover with the egg yolks, milk and sugar. Continue as above.

Shopping reminders:
Grapefruit: grapefruit, sugar.
Casserole of liver: lambs' or calves' liver, streaky bacon, onions, fat, flour, canned baked beans, canned tomatoes, seasoning, stock cube (optional), sugar (optional), potatoes, sprouts.
Queen of puddings: cake or bread, eggs, sugar, milk, jam or fruit purée.

Meals that you can prepare in advance

There are many meals you can prepare in advance and leave to be served or heated when you return. The number of dishes that come under this category is almost endless, so suggestions only are given in this chapter.

For the first course
A first course is not essential, but it helps to turn a simple meal into one that is more satisfying and interesting.

Some of the hors d'oeuvre you can prepare in advance are:

Salads: There are a number in this book and you can create others, using the foods that are in season. Arrange on the plates or dishes, cover tightly with polythene or foil and store in the refrigerator.

Fruit juices, etc.: prepare the fresh fruit juices and put into a cool place. Prepare grapefruit or melon and keep in a cool place.

Pâté: There are many recipes for pâté, but the following is particularly easy and very delicious. Pâté is a highly perishable food, so store carefully.

Liver and tongue pâté [F]

cooking time: 10 minutes

you will need for 6–8 servings:

12 oz. calf's liver	2 tablespoons thick
2 oz. butter	cream
1 small onion	1 tablespoon brandy
6 oz. cooked tongue	(optional)
seasoning	pinch mixed herbs

1 Cut the liver into neat strips and cook in the hot butter very slowly until tender, do not allow to become hard on the outside. The onion should be peeled and halved and put into the pan with the liver, to give a delicate flavour, then it can be removed.
2 Mince the liver and tongue finely and blend with seasoning, the cream, brandy and herbs.
3 Put into a container, put a plate and weight on top and leave until cool and firm.

To vary:
Blender pâté (*liver and tongue*) [F]
Put the liver, tongue, and all ingredients gradually into the blender and switch on until smooth. You may find you need to add a little extra liquid, or use any butter left in the pan as liquid – if the mixture is too stiff the blades in the blender cannot revolve.

Chicken liver pâté [F]
Use chickens' livers instead of calf's liver.

Garlic pâté [F]
Add 1–2 crushed cloves of garlic to the mixture.

Soups

If you make the soup in advance it just needs heating through. If the recipe contains a lot of milk or cream, which might cause the soup to burn easily it is quite a good idea to put this into the top of a double saucepan and heat over boiling water.

One of the easiest of soups is to grate a selection of fresh vegetables (allow about 12 oz.) and simmer these in 1½ pints chicken stock; they will be tender and still full of flavour within about 15 minutes. Season well and top with fresh cream before serving.

Fish dishes

Fish is not an ideal food to prepare in advance for it deteriorates quickly unless it can be stored in a refrigerator.

However, many fish dishes can be got ready early to save last minute preparation, e.g.
Fish salads or spiced fish, see recipe for spiced herrings, below.
Fish cakes and fish pies, see pages 6, 29 and 54.
Fish stews, see recipe on page 64.

Spiced herrings

cooking time: 35–45 minutes

you will need for 4 servings:

4 large or 8 small	1 teaspoon sweet
herrings	spice
1 small onion	2 bay leaves
1 unpeeled dessert	¼ pint water
apple	¼ pint vinegar
1 teaspoon pickling	
spice	

1 If the fishmonger has not prepared the herrings, cut off heads and bone. To do this split along stomach and open out herrings, lay fish flat with cut side downwards and run your fingers along back *very vigorously.* Turn fish over and you will find the backbone easily lifts out.
2 Roll the fish and place in a casserole.
3 Slice the onion and unpeeled dessert apple.
4 Add the rest of the ingredients to the casserole, cover.
5 Cook, if small herrings for 35 minutes or if large for 45 minutes, in centre of very moderate to moderate oven (350–375°F., Gas Mark 4–5).
6 Serve hot or cold with salad.

To cook in a pressure cooker
Put into a pressure cooker instead of a casserole, bring to 15 lb. pressure and cook for 5–6 minutes, depending upon the size of the herrings. To make sure the fish is not over-cooked cool the cooker rapidly, following the manufacturer's instructions.

To vary:
Spiced white fish
Ingredients as spiced herrings, but omit the apple and use 1–1¼ lb. (weight without bone)

63

of firm white fish – hake, halibut, turbot or cod are ideal.

Cut the fish into neat fingers and proceed as stages 3–6. The cooking time will be approximately 35 minutes.

Spiced mackerel

Use mackerel instead of herrings and cook for 45–50 minutes.

Fish Stew

cooking time: 20 minutes plus
                 25 minutes reheating

you will need for 4 servings:

2–3 rashers bacon	seasoning
1–2 medium onions	1¼ lb. white fish –
2 oz. margarine *or*	choose one with
butter	a firm flesh –
1 oz. flour	hake, cod,
¾ pint fish stock,*	halibut or turbot
see below, *or*	or tuna fish.
chicken stock.	

*made by simmering fish skins and bones in water or by flavouring water with anchovy essence.

to garnish:

chopped parsley

1 Remove the rinds from the bacon and cut into neat pieces.
2 Peel and chop the onions and toss both the bacon and the onions in the margarine for about 5 minutes.
3 Stir in the flour and cook for several minutes, then gradually blend in the stock.
4 Bring to the boil and cook until thickened. Season well, but avoid using too much salt if you have used anchovy essence to flavour the stock.
5 Cut the fish into neat fingers, add to the hot sauce and cook for 5 minutes only, then put into a casserole and cover with foil.

To reheat:
Put into a moderate oven, just above the centre (350–375°F., Gas Mark 4–5) and heat for 25 minutes. Remove foil and top with parsley.

To vary:
Add small can sweetcorn.

Add 2–3 skinned chopped tomatoes at stage 2. Top with creamed potatoes instead of foil and heat for 30–35 minutes to brown potatoes as well as heat the fish stew.

Meat and poultry dishes

Roast meat is perhaps the least successful type of meat to prepare in advance.

Obviously you can prepare the stuffing and many people do roast the meat earlier, slice it and reheat in the gravy, but both flavour and texture are lost if this is done. There are, however, all kinds of other meat and poultry dishes that can be prepared in advance, for example:

STEWS AND CASSEROLE dishes are excellent if they are cooked completely and reheated as required. Most people agree that a casserole dish that is reheated for the second time tastes better than when cooked for the first time. If preferred, however, the casserole or stew may just be prepared and cooked when needed.

It must be stressed, however, that when reheating a stew or casserole dish it MUST be heated thoroughly on the second occasion, no matter how well cooked it was originally – many cases of food poisoning have been traced to inadequately heated stews, gravies, etc.

As an example of a stew you will find Rice and beef stew and Chicken à la king on page 65.

Meat puddings, such as steak and kidney pudding, can be cooked for a minimum of 2½ hours, until the pastry is completely set and light, then reheated for the rest of the time when needed. Meat pies and patties can generally be prepared, stored in a cool place, and baked as required. Chicken and pepper patties on page 66 are one example.

All kinds of rissoles or other dishes made with ready cooked meats can be prepared, then fried or baked just before the meal. A basic recipe for rissoles with some variations is on page 67.

Rice and beef stew [F]

cooking time: about 2½ hours

you will need for 4–5 servings:

1½ lb. stewing steak	1 pint stock *or* water
1 oz. flour	and 2–3 beef
¼ teaspoon pepper	stock cubes
½ teaspoon salt	1 teaspoon
2 oz. fat	Worcestershire
2 large onions	sauce
1 clove of garlic	small can peas *or*
4 tomatoes	packet frozen peas
	(or peas and
	carrots)
	3 oz. long grain rice

1 Cut the meat into small pieces and coat with the flour, to which has been added the pepper and salt.
2 Heat the fat in a saucepan, lightly brown the sliced onions and crushed garlic, then the meat.
3 Add the skinned, sliced tomatoes, stock or water and stock cubes, and Worcestershire sauce.
4 Cover and simmer for about 2 hours until the meat is nearly tender, check there is still approximately 1 pint liquid, if necessary add additional stock or water.
5 Add peas and rice, cook for 20 minutes longer, stirring once or twice as the mixture thickens.
6 Serve with green salad.

Note: the stew may be prepared the day before up to stage 5, then reheated and peas and rice added.

To use a pressure cooker for stews

A pressure cooker saves a great deal of cooking time for stews.

If using this recipe you would follow stages 1–3 using the pressure cooker as an ordinary saucepan, but cutting the amount of liquid down to ¾ pint, as there is less evaporation in a pressure cooker. You would then put on the lid, bring to 15 lb. pressure, following the manufacturer's instructions carefully, and cook for 15 minutes if the meat is good quality, or cut into fairly small pieces and cook for 20 minutes if less good quality or larger pieces. Allow the pressure to drop gradually at room temperature. Then add the peas and rice and again use the pan as an ordinary saucepan, cooking for 20 minutes as the basic recipe OR bring once more to pressure and allow 3 minutes only. Allow pressure to drop at room temperature and serve.

To vary:

Use lamb chops from loin or best end of neck and simmer for 1 hour at stage 4, or use middle neck of mutton and allow 1½ hours.

Vary the selection of flavouring vegetables – add mushrooms, sliced green and red pepper.

Add additional flavourings – curry powder, mixed herbs, few drops chilli sauce, etc.

Chicken à la king

cooking time: 20 minutes plus
45 minutes reheating

you will need for 4 servings:

12 oz. cooked	¼ pint chicken stock
chicken	*or* water and half
2 oz. butter *or*	chicken stock
margarine	seasoning
2 oz. flour	1 green pepper
½ pint milk	medium can sweet-
	corn

to serve:

sausagemeat balls	mushrooms
fried bread triangles	

1 Cut the chicken into neat pieces.
2 Heat the butter in a large saucepan.
3 Stir in the flour and cook for several minutes.
4 Gradually add the milk and stock, or water and stock cube, and seasoning.
5 Bring to the boil and cook until you have a smooth sauce.
6 Meanwhile cut the pepper into strips, put in boiling water for about 5 minutes.
7 Drain, add to the sauce with the drained sweetcorn and chicken.
8 Put into a casserole, cover with foil.

To reheat:

Put in the centre of a very moderate oven (325–350°F., Gas Mark 3–4) for approximately 45 minutes. If wishing to keep hot, lower the heat. Stir before serving.

To vary:

Paprika chicken

Omit the canned sweetcorn, and use red instead of green pepper. Blend 1–2 teaspoons paprika pepper with the flour at stage 3.

Chicken blanquette

Omit both the pepper and the corn. Cut 2–5 oz. button mushrooms into neat strips and fry in 1 oz. butter. Add to the mixture at stage 7, together with the chicken, the finely grated rind of 1 lemon and ¼ pint thin cream.

Sausagemeat balls

cooking time: few minutes
reheating 45 minutes

you will need for 4 servings :

8 oz. pork sausage-meat	1 egg yolk
1 tablespoon chopped parsley	½ teaspoon chopped fresh herbs *or* pinch dried herbs

to coat:

1 egg white	1 oz. crisp bread-crumbs (raspings)

to fry:

1 oz. fat

Mix all the ingredients together and form into about 8 small balls.
Coat these in egg white.
Then roll in the crumbs.
Fry for a few minutes in the hot fat.

To reheat:

Lift out of the fat and put in a shallow dish. Reheat in the coolest part of the oven.

Mushrooms

Cut 4–6 oz. mushrooms in slices, having washed and dried them thoroughly. Toss in 2 oz. butter or margarine, put into a shallow ovenproof dish and heat through in the oven.

Fried bread triangles

Cut slices of bread, remove the crusts if wished, then cut into triangles. Heat a little fat in a frying pan and fry the bread until just golden and crisp – do not over brown if you are reheating these. Lift out of the pan and put on to an ovenproof dish or plate.

Fried bread may be reheated in a cool part of the oven for approximately 10–15 minutes which regains its crispness, but it should be drained for a few minutes on absorbent paper.

Chicken and pepper patties

cooking time: 35 minutes

you will need for 4 servings :

8 oz. short crust
pastry *or* 12 oz.
ready-prepared
short crust

for the filling:

10–12 oz. cooked chicken	2 large tomatoes
1 red pepper (fresh or canned)	1 large onion seasoning

to glaze:

1 egg

1 Roll out the pastry and cut into about 8 large rounds.
2 Chop the chicken into neat pieces.
3 Chop the pepper into small pieces. If using fresh pepper this should be put into boiling water for 5 minutes after chopping to 'blanch' or soften.
4 Skin and chop the tomatoes, peel and chop the onion very finely or grate this coarsely.
5 Blend all ingredients together and season well.
6 Put spoonfuls of the mixture on to the rounds of pastry, brush edges with water, then fold over (like a Cornish pasty), seal and flute the edges.
7 Put on to baking trays, brush with beaten egg.
8 Bake for 20 minutes in the centre of a hot oven (425–450°F., Gas Mark 6–7), then lower the heat slightly for the remainder of the cooking time.
9 Serve hot or cold with a mixed salad.

To vary:

Chicken and mushroom patties: use uncooked mushrooms in place of pepper.

Rissoles

cooking time: 20–25 minutes

you will need for 4 servings:

12 oz. cooked
  chicken *or* meat
  or corned beef
2 oz. soft bread-
  crumbs

for the sauce:

1 oz. margarine *or*
  dripping
1 oz. flour

¼ pint brown stock
  or water and ½
  beef stock cube
  seasoning

to coat:

1 egg
2 oz. crisp bread-
  crumbs (raspings)

to fry:

2–3 oz. fat

1 Either mince the meat or chop it very finely, or flake canned corned beef.

2 Mix with the soft crumbs.

3 Make the sauce, then add to the meat and crumbs, season well, allow the mixture to cool.

4 Form into round cakes then coat in beaten egg and crumbs. If the mixture is a little soft to handle coat in seasoned flour before coating in the egg.

5 Fry in hot fat until crisp and golden brown, then drain on absorbent paper.

To vary:

Croquettes

The above recipe can be used and the mixture formed into finger shapes. It is then better to fry in deep fat.

Savoury rissoles

Use all the ingredients as basic recipe, plus 1 medium onion, 2 tomatoes and 2 oz. fat instead of 1 oz. Peel and chop or grate the onion finely and skin and chop the tomatoes. Heat the fat (margarine or dripping as in the original recipe), fry the onion and tomatoes in this, then add the flour and proceed to make the sauce.

The sauce may also be flavoured with mixed herbs; with curry powder; with Worcestershire sauce, or any other savoury sauce.

Shepherd's pie

Prepare the mixture as for savoury rissoles, but do not form into cakes, instead put into a pie dish and top with mashed potatoes (dehydrated potatoes are very good for this). Top with a small amount of margarine to encourage the potatoes to brown and heat for about 30 minutes in a moderately hot oven.

Vegetables

Root vegetables can be scraped or peeled and kept in cold water for a limited time. New potatoes tend to discolour very quickly. Green vegetables lose Vitamin C if left exposed to the air for any length of time, so do not shred cabbage until required. The outer leaves from sprouts can be taken off. Green vegetables can be washed and trimmed and put into polythene bags or boxes in the refrigerator. Peas may be shelled and stored in the same way.

Desserts

Fruit pies and **tarts** may be made in advance, either left unbaked or baked and reheated gently when required.

Stewed fruits, fruit salads of all kinds can be prepared and left in a cool place.

A fruit fool, made with the fruits in season, or with canned or frozen fruits is a simple light dessert to prepare, see recipe below, so are **trifles, jellies,** etc.

Meringues are a useful 'stand-by', for tea or for a dessert. A recipe to make these is on page 68, and they can be used in a variety of ways, e.g.

Meringues glacés: sandwich the two halves of the meringue with ice cream.

Meringues Chantilly: whip thick cream until it holds its shape, flavour with a few drops of vanilla essence and sweeten to taste. Sandwich the meringues with the cream just before serving.

Fruit fool

Cook fruit in season with sugar to taste and the minimum of water. When a thick purée, sieve or beat until smooth, or put into the blender of the mixer. If using canned fruit, drain off surplus syrup and proceed as above.

Blend the fruit purée with an equal amount of whipped cream or thick custard, or use half cream and half custard. Put into glasses and chill thoroughly. Top with cream before serving.

The best fruits to use are: apricots, apples, blackberries, blackcurrants, gooseberries, plums of all kinds (including damsons), rhubarb.

Meringues

cooking time: 1½–3 hours

you will need for about 10–16:

2 egg whites	*or* 2 oz. castor and
4 oz. sugar – all	2 oz. *sieved*
castor sugar *or*	icing sugar
2 oz. castor and	
2 oz. granulated	
sugar, which	
makes a very crisp	
meringue,	

1 Whisk egg whites until *very stiff* – you should be able to turn bowl upside down – *never* add sugar until satisfied the egg whites are stiff.
2 Ways of adding the sugar:

Method a) When whites are stiff, fold in sugar with a metal spoon carefully and gently – this is ideal for a meringue topping on a sweet but NOT good to make into separate meringues.
Method b) When whites are stiff, beat in sugar very gradually adding a dessertspoon at a time – making sure egg whites remain stiff.
Method c) Beat in half sugar, fold in rest – both *b*) and *c*) give firm meringues.
Method d) – with electric mixer. When egg whites are stiff, keep mixer on steady speed, and tip in sugar *gradually* until all is absorbed.
3 Brush baking trays with olive oil or melted butter.
4 Dip a spoon in the egg white mixture – hold over the tray, then with a second spoon turn on to the baking tray giving a neat shape, or put mixture into piping bag with ¼–½ inch pipe and press out into desired shape.
5 For small meringues set for about 1½–2 hours in a very cool oven (225°F., Gas Mark 0–¼), for larger meringues allow up to 3 hours, until crisp but still white.
6 To remove from trays, dip a palette knife in hot water, shake fairly dry, but insert under meringues while still warm. Lift carefully. When quite cold remove from cooling tray – store in airtight tins.

Menus for automatic cookers

The following are some suggestions for meals in automatic cookers with hints to give you the best results.
First read the comments on pages 9 and 10 and those given by your cooker manufacturer. Simple suggestions for making use of your automatic cooker for breakfast will be found on page 26. If you are leaving the meal unattended make quite certain you check the oven setting or temperature with your manufacturer's instructions, as well as those given in this book. Ovens vary very much and you do not wish to spoil the meal. As a precaution temperatures should be kept a little on the 'low side'.

It is also a good idea to use the cooker on automatic setting for the first time when you are at home, so that you can check that *the controls are working properly.*
Things to check when you set the oven automatically.
1 You have set the oven to the right temperature or mark.
2 The main switch is *on* when using electricity and the gas supply is alright.
3 You set *the time you wish the oven to switch on or ignite the gas.*
4 You set *the time you wish the oven to switch off or the gas to be turned off.*

5 *And most important* – make sure the cooker is set to *automatic and not manual.*

Note: The comment 'cooler part of oven' is *not* the floor of a gas cooker.

Meals where roast meat is the main dish

Note: The size of the joint is the most important point to consider, for everything else must fit in with the time allowed for the roast meat.

Menu:
Roast beef
Yorkshire pudding
Roast potatoes
Peas and carrots
Fruit pie

Joints of beef to choose: topside, sirloin. Weight of meat: 3 lb. – this means cooking for 1 hour for under-done meat, up to 1 hour 15 minutes which gives well done meat. The cooking time for all the dishes in this menu, therefore, even when cooked separately, would be 1¼ hours at the temperature given below.
Oven temperature: moderately hot to hot (400–425°F., *Gas Mark* 5–6).

Positions in oven:

Hottest part: **Beef** and **medium sized potatoes.** Roll the potatoes in hot fat and put round the meat – this prevents their becoming dark due to exposure to the air; small to medium sized potatoes need to cook for 1 hour, slightly larger for 1 hour 15 minutes.
Next hottest part: **Yorkshire pudding** – well grease a fairly deep tin, then pour in the batter (recipe page 53). By using a fairly deep tin you delay the cooking time so the pudding is not over-cooked. The pudding will not rise quite as high as in a proper Yorkshire pudding tin and as when cooked in a hot to very hot oven (which is the normal temperature) but it should be crisp, brown and good.
Fruit pie – this should stand next to the

Yorkshire pudding on a small baking tin, which makes sure that any fruit juice will not boil out into the oven. Lay a piece of foil over the pastry so that it does not become too brown.
Cooler part of the oven: put the **diced carrots** and **fresh peas** into a casserole, season well, add a pinch of sugar, and sprig of mint when in season. Cover the vegetables with cold water, add a small knob of butter or margarine to help preserve flavour, and cover the casserole with tightly fitting foil (this is better than a lid).
When you dish up the meal: make the gravy and strain the peas and carrots. Serve with a green vegetable if wished.

Menu:
Stuffed roast chicken, [F] sausages, [F]
  bacon rolls and bread sauce
Roast potatoes
Casserole of celery
Pineapple upside-down pudding [F]

Note: bacon rolls should not be put in the freezer.

Weight of bird: 3 lb. when trussed. Naturally the weight of the stuffing makes this heavier so the total cooking time should be approximately 1¼ hours, or if the bird is slightly bigger then allow 1½ hours, but protect the pudding carefully.
Oven temperature: moderately hot (400°F., *approximately Gas Mark* 5).

Positions in oven:

Hottest part: **Stuffed chicken** with the breast covered with fat to help it brown potatoes for roasting – see previous menu.
Next hottest part: **Sausages** – choose large size and if allowing 1½ hours then cover dish with foil and remove this when you get home so that they can brown more.
Cooler part: **Pineapple upside-down pudding,** see recipe page 70.
Casserole of celery – see recipe page 70.
Bacon rolls: roll the bacon – make these rolls fairly large, put on to ovenproof small plate and cover with foil so that they do not become too crisp and brown.

Bread sauce (recipe page 78) in a gas cooker this can be put on the floor of the oven. To prepare the bread sauce for an automatic oven, pour the hot milk over the crumbs, add the other ingredients and stir well. Put into an ovenproof dish, cover. Stand this in a bowl of cold water and wrap a piece of foil right over the two containers (see instructions for 'steamed' pudding, page 48) or put in a warming drawer. In an electric cooker put into a warming cupboard.

When you dish up this meal: you have no gravy to make, that is with the celery, but a small spoonful of the fat in the roasting tin may be stirred into the celery if desired.

Stuffings to choose for chicken

The most usual stuffing is **veal stuffing,** often called parsley and thyme, and while you can buy this in a packet it is quick to make, particularly if you can put the crumbs and parsley into the blender.

To make enough for a bird of 3 lb. when trussed, i.e. 4 good portions: blend 3 oz. soft breadcrumbs with 1½ oz. shredded suet or melted margarine, ½ teaspoon dried mixed herbs or at least 1 teaspoon freshly chopped herbs (sage, thyme – use more thyme than sage), add up to 1–1½ tablespoons chopped fresh parsley and the grated rind of ½–1 lemon. Bind with 1 egg or, if you are saving egg whites for a meringue, use the yolk only. Add a little lemon juice and enough chicken stock or milk to give a soft consistency. Remember the stuffing will seem very soft if you have melted the margarine.

Pineapple and raisin stuffing

This is delicious, but naturally you would not choose this if having a pineapple upside-down pudding as in the menu above.

Put 2 oz. soft breadcrumbs into a basin, moisten with the juice of ½ lemon. Open a small can of pineapple chunks or chopped pineapple. Drain off the syrup. Add the finely chopped pineapple to the bread, together with 2 oz. chopped walnuts. Moisten 3 oz. seedless raisins with about 4–5 tablespoons pineapple syrup

and allow to stand for 30 minutes, then add the plumped raisins to the crumbs. Lastly add 1 oz. melted butter or margarine.

Sausagemeat stuffing

Blend 8 – 12 oz. sausagemeat with chopped parsley, mixed herbs to taste, and bind with an egg.

The finely chopped liver of the chicken may be added if wished.

Remember **packet stuffings** may be given extra flavour by adding freshly chopped herbs, chopped nuts, celery, etc.

Casserole of celery

First make stock from the giblets of the chicken, or use water and chicken stock cubes. Heat 2 oz. fat in a pan, stir in 1½ oz. flour (or flour and a little gravy browning) then gradually add the stock, use 1 pint. Bring to the boil and thicken, then season well. Cut enough celery for 4 people into neat pieces, put into a casserole, pour sauce over and cover tightly.

Pineapple upside-down pudding [F]

Choose a 7–inch cake tin with a firm base (*not* one with a loose base) or soufflé dish. Spread 1 oz. butter and 1 oz. brown sugar over the bottom of the tin or dish, and grease the sides well. Cover the base with rings of pineapple (allow about 6 rings – cutting these to fit well). The pineapple should be drained from the syrup, but you may then add 2 tablespoons syrup at the bottom of the tin or dish to give a pleasant sauce.

Make a sponge mixture by creaming 4 oz. margarine with 4 oz. castor sugar, add 2 eggs gradually and fold in 6 oz. self-raising flour. Then moisten with 2 tablespoons milk or pineapple syrup and spread over the pineapple. Make sure there is plenty of space for the pudding to rise. Protect the sides of the tin or dish by wrapping in foil and lay a piece of foil over the top of the pudding. When dishing up the chicken, check to see if the pudding is well set, etc. If not brown, remove the foil from the top and leave uncovered while you eat the first course. It is, however, better to protect the pudding as suggested here.

Note: The one-stage method of mixing can, of course, be used successfully for the sponge. Other fruits may be used instead of pineapple.

Menu:
**Roast pork chops, stuffed apples,
  sage and onion stuffing** [F]
**'Oven boiled' potatoes and peas,
  French style**
Fruit crumble

Choose thick loin chops, allow 1 per person.

Oven temperature: moderately hot (400°F., *approximately Gas Mark 5*).
cooking time: 40 minutes.

Positions in oven:

Hottest part: **Chops** in roasting tin with **stuffed apples, sage and onion stuffing** in covered dish with the outside of the dish protected by foil.
Next hottest part: **'Oven boiled' potatoes** – put the peeled potatoes or scraped new potatoes into a casserole, covered with cold water, salted and with a sprig of mint. As the cooking time for this menu is short the potatoes should be very small.
Note: If the onions in the stuffing were fairly well cooked the stuffing could occupy this position, with the potatoes.
Cooler part: **Peas, French style**, see recipe this page.
Fruit crumble, see recipe page 72.
When you dish up this meal: there is no need to make gravy unless your family particularly like this, for the apples, stuffing and the method of cooking the peas all provide a moist result. Strain the potatoes and top with butter and chopped parsley.

[F] *applies to stuffing only.*

Stuffed apples

These make a good sweet dish by themselves or are excellent with pork, instead of making apple sauce.
Choose 4 tiny cooking apples. Core the apples, do not peel, but slit the skin round the outside so the apples do not 'burst'. Fill the centre with a little brown sugar and raisins, and top with a small knob of butter or margarine.

Sage and onion stuffing [F]

Either peel and chop 2 large onions or use the equivalent in dehydrated onions. If using fresh onions cover with cold water and simmer for 15 minutes, or a little longer if you wish them to be almost cooked. Season lightly as they cook. Strain the onions but keep the stock. Blend onions with 2 oz. soft breadcrumbs, 1 teaspoon dried sage or 2 teaspoons freshly chopped sage, 1 oz. shredded suet or butter or margarine. Season very well. Either bind with an egg or some of the onion stock.
If using dehydrated onions then put into a basin, pour over boiling water and leave for 15 minutes, then proceed as above.

Peas, French style

Line a casserole with damp lettuce leaves, use the outer leaves and save the heart for salad. Put a large packet frozen peas on top with seasoning, a good knob of butter and a thinly sliced onion or a few spring onions. (In this menu where you already have sage and onion stuffing you may care to omit the onions.) Cover with more damp lettuce leaves and well buttered foil.
To serve: You can either lift away the lettuce and just serve the peas, or serve the cooked lettuce and peas together. There is a 'buttery' liquid that can be strained away, or served with the peas, as wished.

Fruit crumble

There is one recipe for fruit crumble on page 58, but this is the more usual one.

cooking time: approximately 40 minutes, see method

you will need for 4 servings:

can fruit pie filling *or* about 1 lb. fruit
very little water, see method

sugar to taste

for the crumble:

3 oz. flour, plain *or* self-raising

1½ oz. margarine
2–3 oz. sugar

1 Either put the fruit pie filling into the dish, or put the fruit in the dish and add required amount of water. Soft fruits need no water, harder fruit needs about 3–4 tablespoons. If the fruit mixture becomes too soft the crumble sinks and does not crisp. Add sugar to taste.

2 Put the flour into a basin, rub in the margarine until the mixture looks like fine breadcrumbs, add the sugar.

3 Press this on top of the fruit mixture. Unless cooking hard plums there is no need to warm the fruit first.

4 Normally one bakes this in the middle of the oven, and in an electric oven that is generally the coolest part. Bake for approximately 40 minutes in a moderate oven but if using a slightly hotter oven, as in the automatic menu above, then

   a) choose the oven position carefully;

   b) place a piece of foil loosely over the crumble, which prevents it becoming too brown, and look at it when you dish up the pork chops; if quite brown leave the foil in position, but if pale remove the foil and let the crumble brown while you eat the first course.

5 Serve hot.

Note:

The above menus assume you have *three shelves* or cooking positions in your oven. Where only *two shelves* or two cooking positions are available you will need either to omit a dish or arrange the dishes on the two shelves. If, however, you feel that the position in the oven is a little hotter than you would choose, you can slow up the cooking by wrapping the container or covering the top of it with foil. The foregoing are three menus using two different heats. If the oven is set at moderately hot to hot you could use this for roasting a variety of meats or poultry, for making meat pies, or cooking desserts like a fruit pie.

An automatic meal simply means selecting those kinds of dishes that need approximately the same oven temperature. It also means that you cook foods in the oven which normally you would cook in a saucepan – for example the oven-boiled potatoes – and you can use the same idea for steaming puddings, as below:

To '*oven steam*' a sponge or other light pudding –

Choose a recipe that takes approximately 1¼–1½ hours to steam. There is a basic recipe on page 48. Follow this recipe, but instead of cooking in small castle pudding tins put into a greased basin with the syrup or jam at the bottom of the basin, and make sure you allow plenty of room for the pudding to rise during cooking.

Cover the pudding in the usual way with just a sheet of greased greaseproof paper, stand the pudding in a larger basin with as much cold water as possible – do not over-fill as the water will boil out into the oven. Put a double thickness of greaseproof paper or a sheet of foil over both basins, and either 'tuck in' very firmly round the edges or tie firmly with string. The object of this is to prevent the water in the outer basin from evaporating.

Pastry making

Many recipes need pastry, but if you have no time to make your own, remember there are very good ready-made pastries available. Your baker may have puff or short crust pastry to buy, or these may be purchased frozen, or one can obtain pastry mixes.

If you buy frozen puff or short crust pastry: store as directed on the packet; should you own a home freezer it is an excellent idea to keep packets of ready-made pastry or well wrapped home-made pastry in your deep freeze. This can be taken out, thawed sufficiently to roll out, then used as ordinary pastry.

Do not allow the pastry to become too soft before you roll it out, otherwise it is sticky and needs too much flour on the pastry board or rolling pin.

If using packet pastry follow directions for mixing and baking.

It is possible, however, to make pies and flans with mixtures other than the usual pastry mixtures, and these are often useful to the busy housewife. Some suggestions will be found after the pastry recipes.

Short crust pastry [F]

cooking time: as individual recipe

you will need:

8 oz. plain flour	4 oz. fat (margarine,
pinch salt	butter, *or*
	½ margarine,
	½ cooking fat)

1 Sieve flour and salt.
2 Rub in fat until like fine breadcrumbs.
3 Mix with cold water to a firm rolling consistency.

Variations:

Rich short crust pastry [F]– use all butter. You can use up to 5 oz. Blend with egg yolk and water.

Sweet short crust pastry [F] – add 1 oz. sugar to flour. Blend with egg yolk and water.

Flan or fleur pastry

cooking time: as individual recipe

you will need:

5 oz. butter	pinch salt
1 oz. sugar	1–2 egg yolks
8 oz. flour	water

1 Cream butter and sugar together until light.
2 Sieve the flour and salt together, and add to the creamed butter, mixing with a knife.
3 Gradually add enough egg yolks to make a firm rolling consistency, or use 1 egg yolk and a little water.
4 Roll out and use as instructed in individual recipes.

Puff pastry [F]

cooking time: as individual recipe

you will need:

8 oz. plain flour	few drops lemon
pinch salt	juice
cold water to mix	7–8 oz. butter *or*
	margarine

1 Sieve flour and salt, then mix to a rolling consistency with water and lemon juice.
2 Roll to an oblong shape.
3 Make fat into neat block and place in centre of pastry and fold over it first the bottom section of pastry and then the top section, so that the fat is quite covered.
4 Turn dough at right angles, seal edges and 'rib' carefully, then roll out.
5 Fold dough into envelope, turn, seal edges, 'rib' and roll again.
6 Repeat five times, so making seven rollings and seven foldings in all.
7 Rest the pastry in a cold place once or twice between rollings, to prevent it becoming sticky and soft.
8 Always rest it before rolling for the last time, and before baking.
9 Bake in a very hot oven (475°F., Gas Mark 8) for the first 10–15 minutes, then reduce heat to moderate (375°F., Gas Mark 4) to finish cooking.

Flaky pastry [F]

cooking time: as individual recipe

you will need:

8 oz. flour	5–6 oz. fat
pinch salt	water to mix

1 Sieve flour with salt.
2 Divide fat into three portions and rub one portion into flour.
3 Mix to a rolling consistency with cold water and roll out to oblong shape.
4 Cut second portion of fat into small pieces and lay on two thirds of the dough, leaving remaining third without fat.
5 Fold two of the corners over second third to make an 'envelope' with its flap open.
6 Fold over the top end of pastry, so closing the envelope.
7 Turn pastry at right angles and seal open ends.
8 'Rib' at intervals with a rolling pin to give a corrugated effect, thus equalising the pressure of air and so making certain the pastry will rise evenly.
9 Repeat the process using the remaining fat and turning pastry in same way.
10 Roll out once more and put into a cold place for 30 minutes if it feels very soft and sticky.
11 Fold pastry as before, turn, seal edges and 'rib' again.
12 Altogether the pastry should have three foldings and three rollings.
13 Stand in a cold place for a little while, before baking, to make the pastry rise better.
14 Cooking temperatures and times are given in individual recipes, but as a general rule bake in a very hot oven (475°F., Gas Mark 8) for the first 15 minutes, then lower the heat to Gas Mark 5–6, or turn an electric oven off to finish cooking.

A new look to flans and pies

Instead of making pastry, try biscuit or other crumb crusts. These can be moulded into flan shapes or pressed over fruit for a pie.

Biscuit crumb crust

Cream 3 oz. butter or margarine with 3 oz. sugar and 3 teaspoons golden syrup.
Add 6 oz. crushed biscuit crumbs (these can be any flavour as desired).

for a flan: mould into a flan shape or press into a 7–8-inch flan ring on an upturned baking tray.
Either stand for several hours in a cool place until firmly set, or bake for 15 minutes in the centre of a very moderate to moderate oven (350–370°F., Gas Mark 4–5). Cool thoroughly before using. Fill with:
a) well drained cooked or canned fruit *to glaze:* blend 2 level teaspoons cornflour or arrowroot with $\frac{1}{2}$ pint syrup from the can, or from the cooked fruit. Boil until thick and clear. Stir well. Cool slightly, then brush or spread over the fruit.
b) ice cream and hot chocolate sauce.
c) canned pie fillings topped with whipped cream.

for a pie: put the pie filling or fruit with a little water and sugar into a pie dish.
Press the crumb mixture on top and spread smoothly with a palette knife. Bake for approximately 25–30 minutes in the centre of a very moderate oven (325–350°F., Gas Mark 3–4) until golden brown and the fruit is soft.
The crust is enough for 4–6 servings.

Coconut macaroon crust

Ingredients as biscuit crust but instead of biscuit crumbs use 5 oz. crushed macaroon biscuits and 2 oz. desiccated coconut. Excellent with apricots.

Cornflake crust

Use cornflakes instead of biscuit crumbs.

Rolled oat crust

Use quick-cooking rolled oats instead of biscuit crumbs. This mixture *must* be baked for 20 minutes at least for the flan.

Crushed wheat topping

This is a quick and very good alternative to pastry as a topping for sweet or savoury ingredients.

Sweet wheat crumble topping

cooking time: 25–30 minutes

you will need for 4–6 servings:

3 oz. butter *or* margarine
3 oz. sugar

6 oz. breakfast wheat cereal (Shredded Wheat) flavouring – see below.

1 Cream the butter or margarine and sugar until soft and light.
2 Crush the wheat cereal, see this page, work into the butter and sugar mixture. Sprinkle over the fruit, press gently with a knife to flatten and bake as instructions for biscuit crumbs.

To vary:

For a softer texture add 1 level tablespoon honey or syrup to the butter and use 2 oz. only of sugar; this, or the recipe above, is suitable for all flavours.

Almond flavouring

Add few drops almond essence to the butter and sugar, and 1 oz. chopped blanched almonds to the completed mixture; this is very good over apricots, apples, cherries.

Coconut flavouring

Use 5 oz. crushed wheat and 1½ oz. desiccated coconut.
This is excellent with most fruits.

Spiced flavouring

Blend ½ teaspoon powdered nutmeg, ½ teaspoon powdered ginger with the butter, etc. This is particularly good with apples.

For flans

The wheat mixture can be used for a flan shape, as page 74, (with any of the flavourings above); the better result is given for this if you use golden syrup, as you can mould the softer mixture more readily.

Savoury wheat crumble topping

cooking time: 25–30 minutes

you will need for 4–5 servings:

3 oz. butter *or* margarine
seasoning

dried herbs, optional
6 oz. breakfast wheat cereal

1 Cream the butter with a generous amount of seasoning, in addition to salt and pepper you can use celery salt, cayenne pepper, pinch dry mustard and pinch sage or thyme, etc.
2 Work in the crushed wheat flakes.
3 The topping is then ready to put over the savoury ingredients.

This is a very good topping for
a) cheese and vegetable pie see page 83, instead of creamed potatoes,
b) fish pie, see page 83, instead of the pastry,
c) meat mixtures, such as steak and kidney, instead of the pastry.

To crush biscuits and cereals

Several recipes above require biscuit or cereal crumbs. Making crumbs is simple, but it can make quite a mess if you are not careful.
If you have an electric blender, switch on and then put the biscuits or cereals into this and switch to high speed until evenly crushed. This will give you a very fine crumb. For a coarser crumb, with the motor running, feed the biscuits or cereals into the blender through the hole left in the lid, or with the lid tilted in such a way that you have no possibility of the crumbs being flung out of the goblet by the force of the motor.
Or:
Put the biscuits or cereals on to a sheet of greaseproof paper, cover with a second sheet of greaseproof paper and roll firmly with a rolling pin.
Or:
Simply crush the biscuits or cereals in a bowl with your hands – this is quite adequate if you require coarse crumbs.

Desserts using biscuit and cereal crust

In addition to using these easy crusts for pies and flans they are excellent for other quick desserts. Here are suggestions:

Banana apricot tart

cooking time: 25-30 minutes

you will need for 4–6 servings:

6 medium sized bananas	3 tablespoons apricot jam
1 lemon	

Select any of the crusts on page 75, the most suitable being those with cornflakes or shredded wheat.

1 Prepare the cornflakes or other crust.
2 Press half the mixture into an 8-inch pie plate or shallow ovenproof dish.
3 Peel and halve the bananas, and put on top of the crust.
4 Blend the finely grated lemon rind and juice with the jam.
5 Spread over the bananas, then top with the remaining crust. Make quite sure the bananas are covered.
6 Bake in the centre of a very moderate to moderate oven.
7 Serve hot or cold with ice cream or cream.

To vary:

Date and apple tart

Chop 6 oz. stoned dates. Moisten with 1 tablespoon boiling water, add 1 tablespoon lemon juice, 1 oz. golden syrup and 12 oz. peeled finely sliced apples (weight when peeled). Continue as Banana apricot tart.

Hawaiian tarts

1 Open a medium sized can of pineapple chunks or rings; drain and cut the fruit neatly. Blend with 3 medium sliced bananas. Continue as Banana apricot tart *or*
2 Mix the pineapple with 6–8 oz. peeled chopped apples (weight when peeled) *or*
3 Mix the pineapple with 4–6 oz. mincemeat.

Using bread instead of pastry

Bread can make a very quick substitute for pastry in many dishes. Here are some ideas for you to try.

Croûtons

Instead of topping meat, etc. with pastry and baking in the oven, simply cook the meat in a casserole or saucepan. Meanwhile cut slices of bread about $\frac{1}{2}$ inch thick, then divide each slice into neat $\frac{1}{2}$ inch squares. Fry in hot deep or shallow fat until crisp and golden brown. Drain on absorbent paper. Put the hot meat into a pie or serving dish and cover with the crisp hot croûtons – allow $\frac{1}{2}$–1 slice of bread per person. Rather smaller cubes of bread are ideal to serve on top of soup, they give a contrast in texture and flavour.

Bread tartlets

Cut very thin slices of fresh bread. Roll each slice once or twice with a rolling pin to make them more 'pliable', then spread thinly with softened butter. Press into lightly greased patty or bun tins, bake for 8–10 minutes towards the top of a hot oven (425–450°F., Gas Mark 6–7). Serve hot or cold, filled with sweet or savoury ingredients, e.g.

Savoury fillings:

a) fried chopped bacon and mushrooms
b) cooked vegetables in a thick cheese sauce
c) prawns or other shellfish blended with mayonnaise
d) scrambled eggs

Sweet fillings:

a) well drained fruit, topped with cream
b) ice cream topped with fruit
c) jam, marmalade or curd

Bread rolls

This does not refer to making rolls, as one might imagine from the heading, but to using bread in place of pastry for sausage rolls, etc.

Sausage rolls

As bread browns and crisps much more quickly than pastry, you should use either lightly cooked or canned sausages for these. Cut 1 thin slice of bread from a small loaf per sausage, remove the crusts and butter very lightly then roll round the sausage, or, to make a more interesting shape, lay the sausage diagonally on the bread and roll – this should allow the sausage to protrude at either end, then secure with a wooden cocktail stick, brush the outside of the bread with a little melted butter, put on a baking tray and heat for 8–10 minutes towards the top of a hot oven.

To vary:
Spread the bread with mashed sardines, roll and continue as above – do not butter the bread on the inside as sardines are very rich and oily.
Spread the bread and butter with cream cheese, mixed with chopped mustard pickles (do not use the mustard sauce, just the onions, etc.).

Emergency vol-au-vent cases

One can buy frozen vol-au-vent cases but round bread rolls make an excellent alternative. Cut a neat round out of the top of rolls – soft topped rolls should be chosen (the pieces of roll removed could be crisped for breadcrumbs). Brush the rolls with melted butter and crisp for about 10 minutes in a hot oven then fill with

a) meat, fish, or poultry in a thick sauce
b) heated canned beans, topped with grated cheese
c) mashed sardines topped with scrambled egg, or chopped hard-boiled egg
d) mashed canned salmon, or tuna blended with grated or chopped cucumber or gherkins

Making savoury sauces

You will find a selection of ready prepared sauces in most grocers and supermarkets. These can be heated as instructions to serve with vegetables, pasta, etc.
There will be occasions, however, when you will need to make your own sauces, and remember that a white sauce or flavoured white sauce is an excellent way of adding the food value of milk to a meal.

To make a sauce:

The recipe for the well known method of making *white sauce* is given below; this one first cooks the butter (or margarine) and flour to form a 'roux'.
For many years it was accepted that one should stir the liquid into the 'roux' slowly, bring to the boil and cook until thickened, but when in a hurry you will find you can produce a perfectly smooth sauce by one of two methods:

a) use the 'roux' method, add all the liquid and whisk the sauce when the liquid comes to the boil – it should give a smooth sauce providing the 'roux' has been well cooked. *If the sauce is slightly lumpy* – whisk very hard or put into an electric blender

b) use the 'blending method', where the flour

or cornflour is blended with the milk – see the second recipe.

White sauce—roux method

cooking time: 5–8 minutes

you will need:

1 oz. butter *or* margarine
1 oz. flour *or* ½ oz. cornflour
½ pint milk for coating consistency (i.e. to use as sauce)

or ¼ pint milk for panada or binding consistency (to make croquettes, etc.)
or 1 pint milk for thin white sauce (for soups)
seasoning

1 Heat the butter gently, remove from the heat and stir in the flour.
2 Return to the heat and cook gently for a few minutes so that the 'roux', as the butter and flour mixture is called, does not brown.
3 Again remove from the heat and gradually blend in the cold milk.
4 Bring to the boil and cook, stirring with a wooden spoon until smooth. Add all the cold milk, bring to the boil, then whisk sharply with a flat egg whisk until quite smooth.
5 Season well. If any small lumps have formed, whisk sharply.

White sauce – blending method

Ingredients as page 77

1 Blend the flour with the cold milk.
2 Put into the saucepan, and stir as the sauce comes to the boil and thickens.
3 Add the butter or margarine and seasoning and continue cooking until quite smooth.

Note: make quite certain that the sauce is adequately cooked, otherwise one has the taste of uncooked flour or cornflour.

To vary:

Cheese sauce: recipe as above, but stir in 3–6 oz. grated cheese when sauce has thickened and add a little mustard.

Parsley sauce: recipe as above but add 1–2 teaspoons chopped parsley.

Hard-boiled egg sauce: make white sauce as above, add chopped hard-boiled eggs.

Mushroom sauce: recipe as above, but before making sauce, simmer 2–4 oz. chopped mushrooms in the milk until tender.

Mint sauce [F]

you will need:

6 tablespoons mint leaves	2 tablespoons vinegar *or* a little hot water and vinegar
1–2 oz. sugar	

Wash and dry the mint leaves and chop finely. If the sugar is put on the chopping board it is much easier to chop the leaves. Put into a basin and mix with the vinegar or hot water and vinegar. The adding of hot water tends to bring out the flavour of the mint.
Transfer to a sauce-boat.

Blending method:

Put all the ingredients into electric blender. Switch on until mint is evenly chopped, then tip into sauce-boat, stand a while as the sauce looks cloudy when first made.

Bread sauce [F]

cooking time: few minutes

you will need for 8 servings:

1 onion	4 oz. breadcrumbs
4 or 5 cloves, if liked	2–4 oz. margarine
1 pint milk	salt, pepper

1 Peel the onion and if using cloves, stick these firmly into the onion.
2 Put into milk, together with other ingredients.
3 Slowly bring to the boil.
4 Remove from heat and stand in a warm place for as long as possible.
5 Just before the meal is ready, heat the sauce gently, beating it with a wooden spoon.
6 Remove the onion before putting into sauce-boat.

Quick ways to prepare bread sauce

1 Put a 4 oz. *slice of bread* (without crusts) in the saucepan with the milk, heat for 5 minutes then beat hard with a wooden spoon. The bread should be fairly stale for this method, fresh bread does not crumble as easily.
2 Use the blender for making the crumbs.

To make gravy

Thin gravy

1 Pour away practically all the fat from the roasting tin, leaving the residue of meat to give flavour.
2 Add about 1 teaspoon flour and approximately ½ pint stock, or water flavoured with meat or vegetable extract, or stock cube.
3 Bring to the boil, cook until clear and strain.

Thickened gravy

1 Leave about 1 tablespoon fat in the meat tin.
2 To this add approximately 1 oz. flour.
3 Cook, stirring, until browned.
4 Add just over ½ pint stock, or water flavoured with meat or vegetable extract, or a stock cube.
5 Bring to the boil, cook until thick and strain.

Brown sauce – roux method

cooking time: 5–8 minutes

you will need:

1 oz. butter *or* margarine	*or* ¼ pint brown stock for panada or binding consistency
1 oz. flour *or* ½ oz. cornflour	
½ pint brown stock for coating consistency (i.e. to use as sauce)	*or* 1 pint brown stock for thin brown sauce seasoning

Make as white sauce, roux method.

Brown sauce – blending method

Prepare as white sauce made in this manner.

To vary brown sauce:

With vegetables: increase the amount of fat to 2 oz. and fry a grated onion or finely chopped onion in the fat before adding the flour.

Madeira sauce

As brown sauce, but use approximately half stock and half Madeira wine. This is made more interesting to serve with meats such as tongue if you add a tablespoon of redcurrant jelly. This gives a faintly sweet flavour which blends well with ham or tongue.

Mixed vegetable sauce

Make the brown sauce in the usual way and then add a medium sized packet of frozen mixed vegetables and heat these in the sauce. A tablespoon of sherry can be included. This is an excellent way of heating slices of cooked tongue, beef, etc.

Port wine sauce

Omit a little stock and use port wine to flavour. This is a very good sauce with duck or for heating jointed chicken, slices of beef, etc.

Orange sauce

Simmer the peel of 2 oranges in a little brown stock for about 5 minutes. Take out the peel, then use the orange juice and brown stock to make a sauce instead of all stock. The orange sauce should be slightly sweet, so add sugar to taste. You may also make this richer by adding a small quantity of port wine.

This is an excellent sauce to serve with duck, and while there are many more complicated recipes, this one gives a very good flavour.

Tomato brown sauce

This is a very pleasant sauce to use in casserole dishes. The quickest way of preparing it is to use half brown stock and half tomato juice.

Cumberland sauce

cooking time: 15 minutes

you will need for 4–6 servings:

grated rind and juice 1 large lemon	1 teaspoon cornflour *or* arrowroot
grated rind and juice 2 large oranges	2 tablespoons port wine
¼ pint water (or half water and half red wine)	2–3 tablespoons redcurrant or apple jelly

1 Put the grated rinds into a saucepan with the water or water and wine. Simmer gently for about 5 minutes until the rind is tender, tightly covering the pan so the liquid does not evaporate.
2 If wished, strain the liquid (which will have absorbed the flavour from the rinds) and discard the rinds, or use the rinds and liquid.
3 Blend cornflour or arrowroot with the juice from the lemon and oranges, add to the liquid (or liquid and rinds) in the pan with port wine and redcurrant jelly.
4 Bring to the boil and cook, stirring well, until thickened and clear.

To vary:

Savoury Cumberland sauce: add a little salt, pepper and made-mustard to taste.

Cherry Cumberland sauce: add approximately 3 tablespoons halved, stoned, fresh ripe cherries or canned cherries, and use the liquid from the can in place of water. This is particularly good with boiled bacon or ham.

Quick barbecue sauce

cooking time: 25–30 minutes

you will need for 5-6 servings

5 tablespoons olive or cooking oil*
1 medium onion, chopped
1 heaped tablespoon sugar
½-1½ tablespoons Worcestershire sauce**
½-1 tablespoon mixed mustard – English or French
½ teaspoon salt
pinch pepper
juice of 1 lemon
6 tablespoons tomato ketchup
6 tablespoons water

*This amount of oil is excellent for keeping meat moist as suggested in the method, but it could be reduced to 2½–3 tablespoons if a less rich sauce is required.

**tastes vary considerably as to how much sauce is liked, use the smaller amount, taste and increase as desired.

1 Heat the oil and cook the onion in it until soft, then add the remaining ingredients.
2 Simmer for 15 minutes. Makes ½ pint.

This is excellent for basting and serving with fried chicken, hot dogs, rissoles, hamburgers. To serve with spaghetti, macaroni or rice dishes allow to simmer rapidly until the sauce thickens.

Snacks and sandwiches

Often the family will have had a very sustaining midday meal and in the evening will need just a snack or selection of sandwiches.

If serving snacks make sure they are not only substantial but varied and well balanced nutritionally also.

Pasta or rice dishes make an excellent one-course meal; follow them with fresh fruit, or serve a salad with them so that the meal is not too starchy.

Many of the egg dishes found in the first breakfast section of the menus are equally suitable for a light snack.

Cheese dishes, of which there is a number in this book, are ideal for a light snack.

Pasta Dishes

The term 'pasta' describes those foods like macaroni, spaghetti, etc. of which a wide variety can be obtained in good grocers, super-markets or delicatessen shops. They form the basis of many practical and interesting dishes – and give a feeling of being 'well fed' since they are sustaining foods.

To cook pasta

Pasta can be easily spoiled if incorrectly cooked – the general fault being overcooking or too little water – remember:
a) Use a good sized pan.
b) Use at least 2 pints water, plus level teaspoon salt to each 4 oz. pasta.
c) Allow water to boil rapidly *before* pasta is put in.
d) Let water continue to boil fairly quickly during cooking period.
e) Stir *gently* once or twice using fork to lift spaghetti and keep separate.
f) Test at end of recommended cooking time – the pasta is cooked when it feels *just tender* (but still with certain body in it) if you press it against the side of the pan with a fork.
g) Strain through a sieve.
h) Rinse with boiling water to prevent it being sticky. This is not essential if used at once – but a good idea if you want to keep the pasta some little time before using.

Times for cooking pasta

These vary quite a little depending on thickness, type, etc. The quick cooking *elbow length macaroni*, etc. takes approximately 7 minutes cooking from the time the macaroni comes to the boil again in boiling salted water. Ordinary macaroni about 18–20 minutes, ordinary spaghetti about 12–15 minutes.

To cook **longer pasta** like **spaghetti:** while this can be broken *before* cooking, it looks more interesting if cooked in long ribbons. Choose a deep, as well as large pan. Bring water to boil, using at least 2 pints water to each 4 oz. spaghetti. Hold spaghetti upright in boiling water for 1–2 minutes – this softens the part in the water. You can then bend it to allow the rest to go into the water. Lift once or twice during cooking with a fork to keep separate.

Macaroni cheese

cooking time: 50 minutes

you will need for 4 servings:

3 oz. macaroni

for cheese sauce:

1½ oz. butter *or* margarine	seasoning
1½ oz. flour	3–4 oz. grated Cheddar cheese
¾ pint milk	

for the topping:

2 tablespoons fine breadcrumbs	½–1 oz. margarine *or* butter
2 oz. grated Cheddar cheese	

1 Cook macaroni. Meanwhile make cheese sauce (see page 78), then mix cooked strained macaroni and cheese sauce together.
2 Put into a pie dish – top with crumbs, cheese, and the margarine or butter in several small pieces. Either bake for about 25–30 minutes near top of moderate to moderately hot oven (375–400°F., Gas Mark 5–6), or if macaroni and sauce are really hot, brown under a moderately hot grill.

If you prepare this dish a while beforehand use little extra milk to give a thinner sauce, as macaroni absorbs liquid and it does become rather too stiff and 'solid' when not served immediately.

To vary:

Use a large can of spaghetti in tomato sauce; blend into the cheese sauce made as above, then put into a dish. Top with crumbs and cheese and continue as macaroni cheese.

Bacon macaroni cheese: add pieces of crisply fried bacon to the cheese and macaroni mixture (cooked ham, cooked chicken, are also excellent).

Macaroni Florentine: put a layer of cooked well drained spinach at the bottom of the dish, top with macaroni mixture. Heat as above (this gives a complete meal in a dish).

Spaghetti Milanaise

cooking time: 40–45 minutes

you will need for 4 servings:

6 oz. spaghetti *or*
  8 oz. for generous portions

for the tomato sauce: [F]

1 lb. fresh tomatoes *or* medium can plum-shaped tomatoes	½ oz. flour *or* ¼ oz. cornflour
1 oz. butter	½ pint water *or* liquid from can (plus water to make ½ pint)
1 small onion*	
1 rasher bacon	good pinch salt, pepper, sugar
bay leaf	

*or use a good shake of garlic salt

to serve with this:

2–3 oz. grated Parmesan *or* Cheddar cheese

1 Cook spaghetti, and in the meanwhile make the sauce.
2 Skin fresh tomatoes, then heat the butter and toss diced onion and bacon in this – do not brown.
3 Add chopped tomatoes and bay leaf, simmer for 10 minutes.
4 Blend flour or cornflour with ½ pint liquid, add to tomato mixture and simmer gently for about 30 minutes. Stir from time to time, rub through a sieve, add seasoning and sugar and reheat.
5 Cook and strain the spaghetti. Serve on hot plates topped with the tomato sauce and grated cheese.

To vary:

Hasty spaghetti Milanaise: use canned tomato soup as a sauce, or buy spaghetti sauce mix, and follow directions for mixing.

Hasty spaghetti Bolognese: open canned stewing steak and heat, flavour with garlic salt and chopped parsley and a little red wine.

Rice Dishes

Rice is not only an ideal dessert, but can be the basis of many savoury dishes. The following recipes are tasty and are quick and easy to make.

Ham risotto

cooking time: 25–30 minutes

you will need for 4 servings:

2 oz. butter *or* 2 tablespoons olive oil
1 onion
3 large tomatoes
4 oz. mushrooms

6 oz. long grain *or* Italian rice
1 pint chicken stock *or* water and chicken stock cube
6 oz. cooked ham

to serve:

grated cheese

1 Heat the butter or oil in a pan.
2 Fry the peeled chopped onion and skinned sliced tomatoes and the sliced mushrooms until tender.
3 Add the rice and turn in the vegetable mixture.
4 Pour in the stock and stir the rice, etc., in this.
5 Bring just to the boil and simmer in an open pan until the liquid has evaporated. Just before the rice is cooked, add the diced ham.
6 To serve, top with grated cheese.

To vary:

Cheese risotto: omit ham, add diced cheese before serving.
Fish risotto: omit ham, add shellfish or diced uncooked fish to the rice mixture, cook until tender. Top with strips of green pepper.
Liver risotto: add diced calf's or chicken's livers to rice mixture.

Cheese Dishes

Cheese is not only an excellent protein food, but very satisfying as well – you feel you have had a good meal when you have eaten cheese. One of the simplest of all snacks is just to serve cheese with rolls, butter, salad and fresh fruit. This is a meal that can be prepared within minutes and varied with different cheeses.

Cheese on toast

Cover slices of buttered toast with slices of Cheddar, Cheshire, Emmenthal, Gruyère or Dutch cheese. Heat under the grill until the cheese has melted.

To vary:

Top the cheese with a lattice of strips of bacon rashers and brown under the grill.

Put slices of ham under the cheese and heat until the ham is warmed through and the cheese melted.

Cover the toast with well seasoned, mashed sardines, then slices of cheese.

Welsh rarebit

cooking time: 10 minutes

you will need for 4 servings:

2 oz. butter
1 oz. flour
¼ pint cold milk
salt and pepper
1 teaspoon made-mustard

8 oz. grated Cheddar cheese
1 tablespoon beer, ale *or* few drops Worcestershire sauce
4 slices bread

Prepare mixture by melting half the butter in a pan, stir in flour, cook for few minutes then gradually add milk. Bring to boil, cook till smooth and thick, add seasoning, most of cheese and beer. Heat steadily until cheese has melted. Toast bread, then butter and spread with the mixture and remainder of cheese. Put under hot grill until brown.

To vary:

The mixture above gives a soft creamy topping – for a firmer mixture use only 4–5 tablespoons milk.

Most people like Welsh rarebit made with Cheddar, Cheshire or Lancashire cheese. A stronger flavour can be given by mixing a little Parmesan with the Cheddar. A very mild flavour is obtained by using a Dutch cheese.

Storing Welsh rarebit

If you are very fond of Welsh rarebit you can make up the mixture as above in larger quantities, store in covered container in refrigerator for a week or so, using as wished.

Buck rarebit

Ingredients as Welsh rarebit, plus
4 poached eggs

Prepare rarebit mixture. Spread on hot buttered toast. Poach the eggs. Put Welsh rarebit under hot grill until brown, then top with the poached eggs, and serve.

Cheese and prawn tarts

cooking time: 15 minutes

you will need for 4 servings:

6 oz. ready-made shortcrust pastry *or* home-made pastry made with 4 oz. flour etc. see page 73	1 oz. Cheddar cheese
	2 eggs
	seasoning
2 oz. frozen prawns *or* canned prawns	

1 Roll out the pastry very thinly, cut in rounds and line 12 patty tins.
2 Chop the prawns, grate the cheese and bind together with the eggs. Season lightly and spoon the mixture into the pastry cases; bake for 15 minutes towards the top of a hot oven (425°–450°F., Gas Mark 6–7).
3 Serve hot or cold.

Cheese and vegetable pie

cooking time: 35-40 minutes

you will need for 4 servings:

for the sauce:

1 oz. butter *or* margarine	seasoning
1 oz. flour *or* ½ oz. cornflour	4 oz. grated Cheddar cheese
½ pint milk	

for the filling:

medium packet frozen mixed vegetables

for the topping:

large packet dehydrated potato *or* approximately 12 oz. mashed potato
1 oz. margarine

1 Make the sauce as recipe page 78.
2 Meanwhile cook and drain the frozen vegetables and blend with the sauce.

3 Put into a pie dish and top with the potato and tiny pieces of margarine.
4 Bake for approximately 25 minutes towards the top of a moderate to moderately hot oven (375–400°F., Gas Mark 4–5) or until the potatoes are brown.

To vary:

Brown under the grill if wished. Top with a cereal crust instead of potato, see page 75. Blend a medium can of corn – creamed or corn kernels – with the cheese sauce and add 4 oz. diced cooked ham.

Use well drained canned vegetables in place of cooked frozen vegetables.

Fish and cheese filling

Blend 4 oz. shelled prawns, or 8 oz. flaked white fish, or canned salmon, with the cheese sauce.

Sandwiches

Ideas for sandwiches

Sandwiches can form the basis of a substantial meal, or they can be small and elegant for tea, supper or a party. There are, however, points to remember to make sandwich preparation quick and easy:

1 Buy wrapped sliced bread if you are short of time, or choose bread that is fresh, not over-fresh. If by chance you are cutting bread and it is very soft and inclined to break, dip your bread knife in hot water, shake dry, but use while warm.
2 If you are not using sliced bread, if you have a lot of sandwiches to prepare, cut the loaf longways.
3 Should the butter or margarine be a little hard, soften it and make it 'go further' by beating in a very little warm milk.

To keep sandwiches fresh

If they are to be used the same day, wrap in foil or greaseproof paper or put into a polythene bag. To keep sandwiches very cool rinse a wide-necked vacuum flask with ice cold water or put in ice cubes and leave for a short time. Tip the ice cubes out very carefully so that you do not crack the interior, and then put in the wrapped sandwiches and close the top. If you wish to prepare sandwiches overnight put the carefully wrapped sandwiches in the salad container of the refrigerator.

To store sandwiches for a longer period, remember sandwiches can be put in the home freezer. Most fillings are suitable for freezing except hard-boiled egg.

Sandwich fillings
Meat fillings [F]:

Curried

Chop cooked meat finely, blend with a little butter and curry powder. Spread the bread more thinly then usual with butter or margarine, put on each slice a crisp lettuce leaf, then the meat filling.

Devilled tomato

Chop cooked meat finely, mix with skinned chopped tomato and a few drops of Worcestershire sauce.

Bacon and cheese

Fry bacon until crisp then chop or crumble and blend with a little cream cheese.

Egg fillings:

with pepper [F]

Scramble eggs lightly, blend with a little salad cream and finely grated cheese (optional) and a little diced green pepper.

with cheese

Chop hard-boiled eggs and blend with a little butter and grated cheese.

with prawns [F]

Scramble eggs lightly, blend with a little salad dressing and chopped shelled prawns.

with curry

Chop hard-boiled eggs coarsely, mix with chopped chives, a pinch of curry powder and a little butter to bind. Use less butter in spreading the bread.

In addition remember that eggs blend with chopped anchovies, mashed sardines, tuna fish, etc.

A soft-boiled egg gives a much more moist filling that a hard-boiled egg. Blend this with butter before spreading.

Cheese fillings:

If Cheddar cheese has become rather hard, grate this and blend with a little mayonnaise or butter for a very moist filling. [F]

Blend grated cheese and mayonnaise with chopped hard-boiled eggs, season well.

Blend grated cheese and mayonnaise, or soft cream cheese, with chopped nuts and raisins. [F]

Add finely chopped green pepper, chopped fresh parsley or chopped chives to cream cheese. [F]

with ham or bacon [F]

Spread the bread and butter very thinly with mustard, cover with crisp lettuce. Either top with slices of cheese (most cheese suitable) with chopped fried bacon or slices of cooked ham, or blend the chopped bacon or ham with grated cheese, adding a little butter or soft cream cheese.

with vegetables [F]

Blend grated raw carrot and cream cheese or grated Cheddar cheese. Make moist with a few drops of milk or mayonnaise.

Whilst tomato and cheese slices and cucumber and cheese slices are familiar mixtures, finely chopped peeled cucumber and strips of tomato pounded into cream cheese also give a delicious moist filling. Grated or cream cheese and cooked shredded beetroot are excellent, but the beetroot does make the bread rather soft and tends to colour this.

with fruit [F]

Blend grated cheese or cream cheese with mashed banana, or with well drained chopped pineapple, or with finely diced dessert apple, or with chopped dates or raisins. (Raisins are made more interesting if sprinkled with a little orange juice and left for a while to absorb this.)

Fish fillings:
with watercress [F]

Blend flaked cooked or canned salmon or canned tuna with finely chopped watercress and a squeeze of lemon juice. Season well. Tuna is inclined to be a little dry, so bind with mayonnaise or well seasoned cream.

with egg

Blend flaked cooked fish, shellfish or canned fish with scrambled or chopped hard-boiled egg and a little grated raw cucumber.

with kippers

Cooked kippers are excellent as a sandwich filling. Since they are rather soft the flesh should be pounded with a little butter and pepper. Mix with chopped egg or shredded lettuce or watercress or cucumber. Any of these counteracts the salt flavour.

with herrings

Freshly cooked, canned or the savoury Bismarck or Rollmop herrings are a good and substantial sandwich filling. With fresh herrings, remove the flesh and pound well with a little butter or mayonnaise, or oil and vinegar and seasoning. With the preserved herrings, drain and pound well. They will probably be sufficiently seasoned. Mix the herrings with chopped hard-boiled egg, or shredded lettuce and shredded cucumber, or gherkin, or with a little very well drained pickled red cabbage, or with grated or chopped dessert apple.

Double decker sandwiches

These are interesting for a main meal or for a party. Choose two fillings that blend well together and yet give a contrast in colour as well as taste. Spread one slice of bread with butter, cover with the first filling, then with a second slice of bread and butter and the second filling, put on the third slice of buttered bread and press together firmly.

Savoury butters [F]

In order to make sandwiches more interesting the butter or margarine used in spreading the bread can be flavoured.

Choose . . . a) **lemon butter** – ideal for fish fillings. Blend the butter with a squeeze of lemon juice and a pinch of finely grated lemon rind, b) **mustard butter** – excellent for any meat or cheese filling. Blend a pinch of dry mustard or a little made English or French mustard with the butter, c) **watercress butter** – ideal for all fillings. Add finely chopped watercress to the butter or margarine with a little lemon juice, d) **herb butter** – use a small amount of freshly chopped herbs, e.g. parsley, mint, chives, lemon thyme, etc., blend with the butter. Providing the right herbs are chosen (for example: mint with a lamb filling) the herb butter is good for most sandwiches, e) **anchovy butter** – blend a few drops of anchovy essence with the butter. Be careful to use less salt in the sandwich filling, particularly good with fish fillings, f) **horseradish butter** – add a little horseradish cream to the butter. Be sparing with pepper in this filling – ideal for meat, particularly beef.

Planning a party

However busy one may be, there is a great pleasure and satisfaction in entertaining friends. Do not regard this as a tiresome and time-consuming 'chore', for it is quite possible to have a party with the minimum of effort. One of the most successful parties is a

Cheese and Wine party

This just means having a good selection of cheeses with rolls or sliced French bread, butter, bowls of apples and crisp celery and wine.

Cheeses to choose:

Allow 6–8 oz. per person. Grocers and supermarkets have such a good selection of cheeses today that you will have no difficulty in making up a good selection.

Buy:

One of the firm traditional cheeses – Cheddar, Cheshire, etc.

A fairly strong flavoured cheese, e.g. Danish Blue, Stilton, etc.

A creamy type of cheese – Brie, Camembert, etc. (make sure it is soft and 'ripe').

A cream or cottage cheese, or if your guests like good flavoured soft cheeses then try a herb or garlic flavoured cheese.
Some processed or mild Dutch cheese – this will be particularly popular with children.

Allow several rolls per person or the equivalent in French bread or biscuits. People vary in the amount of butter they like, but a minimum of 1 oz. should be allowed with biscuits – rather more with bread.
One large head of celery cuts into about 4 portions.

Wine to choose:
In summer time, choose a white wine so that it may be chilled well – a Chablis, dry Graves, a Pouilly Fuissé or a hock.
In winter time, though, a warming red wine blends well with cheese – choose Volnay, Nuits St. Georges, Margaux, Beaune, Mâcon... serve at room temperature.
Follow with good coffee.

Cold Buffet
Many of the savoury dishes in this book are suitable for a buffet party, e.g.
Stuffed eggs, see page 21.
Fish salads, see pages 29 and 50.

With them have large platters of cold meats. Modern supermarkets have wonderful selections, so be adventurous and have a mixture of meats rather than one or two kinds.

Cold meats:
Allow 4–6 oz. per person.
Choose the fairly familiar:
ham, tongue, brisket
add the less well known:
Salami – Italian, Belgian – they all vary in flavour and appearance but are fairly mild on the whole.
Salami – German – these tend to be more strongly flavoured than some.
Liver sausage and pâté.

Salads:
Serve with simple but interesting salads.
Allow 1 oz. each salad per person, have Coleslaw, see next column.

Mixed salad, see page 87.
Potato salad – made by blending cooked potatoes with mayonnaise, chopped chives or grated onion and chopped parsley.
Rice salad – made by blending boiled rice (long grain if possible) with mayonnaise, grated raw carrot, cooked peas, chopped parsley.

Sausage plait

cooking time: 25–30 minutes

you will need for 6 servings:
13 oz. packet frozen puff pastry
1 small egg
12 oz. pork sausage-meat
1 teaspoon basil *or* mixed herbs
seasoning

1 Roll the pastry into an oblong 10 inches long.
2 Break the egg into a cup and beat lightly.
3 Put the sausagemeat, herbs and seasonings into a bowl and mix together; add just enough egg to moisten.
4 Form the sausagemeat into a 4-inch wide roll and place down the centre of the pastry, leaving equal borders each side of the sausage.
5 Gently cut borders obliquely in $\frac{1}{2}$-inch strips to form plait and brush these with remaining egg.
6 Plait alternate strips of pastry over filling (see back cover).
7 Brush with beaten egg to glaze.
8 Bake just above the centre of a hot to very hot oven (450°–475°F., Gas Mark 7–8) for approximately 15 minutes to allow the pastry to rise, then lower the heat for the rest of the time until golden brown.

Some easy salads for families or parties
Quantities are enough for 4 people

Coleslaw: Shred the heart of a small white cabbage and blend with salad dressing. There are many variations on coleslaw: add grated carrot; chopped nuts; drained chopped pineapple; dried fruit; or toss in thin cream flavoured with lemon juice instead of mayonnaise.

Fruit salads: add segments of citrus fruit; peeled diced apple; ripe cherries or other fruit in season, to the more familiar lettuce, etc.

Mixed salad: this could include a great variety of ingredients, lettuce, cress, tomato, cucumber, radishes, hard-boiled egg, etc. Mix the prepared ingredients and toss in oil, vinegar and a little seasoning.
Remember that prepared salads keep moist if covered with foil or polythene in the refrigerator. Do not add oil and vinegar until just ready to serve, though.

Vegetable salads: any left-over cooked vegetables are excellent in salads, particularly beans, peas, carrots, etc. Toss the vegetables in mayonnaise or oil and vinegar while they are warm (if possible) as this gives a pleasantly moist texture, and the vegetables absorb the flavour.

Desserts for a party

There are many desserts in this book suitable for a buffet party; choose those you can prepare beforehand.
Among the most suitable are meringues, page 68, fruit salad, page 48.
Home-made ice cream is another excellent choice or a home-made water ice, and both of these are given below:

Ice cream [F]

There are many ways of making ice cream – you can use ice cream powder (obtainable from supermarkets and grocers) and follow the directions on the tin; you can use all cream, half cream and half custard, or have a base of marshmallows. Since this is both very easy and very excellent in texture, I give this below and also a basic ice cream with cream.
I have given a large quantity for ice creams as they store well for several days in the freezing compartment of the refrigerator, or longer in a home freezer.

Cream ice [F]

no cooking

you will need for 8–9 servings:

½ pint thick cream	flavouring
½ pint thin cream	3 eggs
3–4 oz. sieved icing *or* castor sugar	

If you have a modern refrigerator with 3–star markings, or a home freezer, there is no need to alter the setting before you freeze ice cream or water ices. With an older type of refrigerator, set to the coldest position at least 30 minutes before you freeze the ice cream, then return to normal setting when this is firm. If you have a 1– or 2–star marking on your refrigerator it is still advisable to turn to the coldest position as suggested above.

1 Whip the cream until it just begins to hold its shape, then gradually whisk in the thin cream. The mixture of creams gives a lighter texture than all thick cream.
2 Add the sugar and flavouring, see overleaf.
3 Lastly fold in the stiffly beaten egg whites, if you wish to use the egg yolks see Italian type ice cream below.
4 Put the mixture into the freezing trays, or into an ovenproof dish and freeze. There is no need to whip this ice cream during freezing, providing you make sure with a refrigerator that the freezing compartment is very cold, or have a home freezer, but if you do not mind a little extra trouble you can use the recipe below for 'ultra light' ice cream.

To vary:
Ultra light ice cream: Make as stages 1 and 2, then freeze for about 30 minutes, remove from freezing compartment, whip hard, fold in the stiffly beaten egg whites and re-freeze.
Italian type ice cream: *a)* Use the thick cream and ½ pint custard (made with custard powder, milk and very little sugar) instead of the thin cream.
Italian type ice cream: *b)* Ingredients as cream ice above but the method of making is:

1 Beat the egg yolks and sugar until thick and creamy.

2 Whisk the creams as stage 1, then add the flavouring and fold into the egg yolks and sugar.

3 Fold in the stiffly beaten egg whites and freeze as cream ice.

To flavour cream ice:

Banana: mash 3 ripe perfect bananas with juice of ½ lemon, add to whipped cream.

Chocolate: blend 1½ oz. sieved cocoa or 3 oz. chocolate powder with the whipped cream.

Coffee: blend 2 tablespoons coffee essence with the whipped cream.

Fruit: blend up to ½ pint thick fruit purée (raspberries, etc.) with the whipped cream.

Economy ice cream

Use large can unsweetened evaporated milk instead of the cream. Boil the tin for 15 minutes in a pan of water (cover throughout this time). Allow can to cool, open, pour the milk into a large bowl and whisk until thick.
Continue as cream ice.

Water ice [F]

cooking time: few minutes

you will need for 6–8 people:

1½ pints thick fruit pulp – see method	2 teaspoons powder gelatine
sugar to taste	2 egg whites

1 Sieve the fruit pulp if wished; when using ripe fruit such as raspberries. etc. do not cook; other fruit – plums, etc. should be cooked with the minimum of water. You could use canned fruit purée if wished. Add enough sugar to give a fairly sweet taste – do not over-sweeten though.

2 Heat a small quantity of the pulp and dissolve the gelatine in this. Gelatine is not essential, but it is a very good idea if you intend to keep the ice for a day or two, since it helps to prevent splinters of ice developing.

3 Stir the gelatine into the fruit pulp.

4 Freeze until slightly thickened, then fold in the stiffly whisked egg whites and freeze until firm.

Marshmallow ice cream [F]

cooking time: few minutes

you will need for 8–9 servings:

6 oz. marshmallows	½ pint thick cream
¼ pint milk	¼ pint thin cream
flavouring	sugar – see method

1 Heat the marshmallows over a very gentle heat with the milk, allow to cool after the marshmallows have nearly melted.

2 Whip the thick cream until it just begins to hold its shape, then add the thin cream gradually, and whisk again.

3 Add the melted cooled marshmallows and milk and the flavouring, then freeze as above. Taste before freezing and add a little sugar if not sweet enough.

Use any of the flavourings above, try adding chopped nuts and also well-drained canned pineapple, etc.

Marshmallow cream sponge

no cooking

you will need for 5–6 servings:

1 cream sponge (frozen)	1–2 packets marshmallows

1 Allow to defrost and place cream sponge in a dish.

3 Arrange the marshmallows over the top, then brown lightly under a moderately hot grill.

2 If wished, serve with defrosted frozen strawberries or raspberries.

Chocolate mousse and pears

no cooking

you will need for 4 servings:

15 oz. can pears	4 party shaped tubs chocolate mousse

1 Drain and chop the pears, keeping the juice for another occasion.

2 Arrange chopped pears in a layer at the base of individual glasses.

3 On top of the pears turn out a mousse (as directions on tub). If wished, decorate with whipped cream, angelica and glacé cherries.

A Dinner Party

Many of the menus in this book are suitable for a dinner party. I have included a first course with most menus, and often this may be omitted for the family meal, but included when you wish a more interesting menu.

Choose a dinner party menu where much of the preparations can be done beforehand, i.e. at least one course is made in advance.

Cocktail snacks to make in a hurry

Often one invites friends in for a drink and would wish to serve a cocktail snack with this. It is therefore advisable to keep a supply of potato crisps in an air-tight tin, a jar of gherkins, cocktail onions, tin of salted nuts, and packet of tiny biscuits on which to put various mixtures. The suggestions below, however, are rather more original ideas; each of them will make about 12–16 canapés:

Anchovy fingers

Cut 3 slices of white or brown bread and butter. Spread with anchovy paste. Hard-boil 2 eggs, chop the whites and yolks separately and arrange lines of egg white and egg yolk over the anchovy paste. Cut into neat fingers.

Avocado and cream cheese canapés

Halve a ripe avocado pear, remove the stone and scoop out the pulp. Put this into a basin, add a tablespoon of lemon juice and 2 oz. cream cheese. Season lightly, spread on crisp small biscuits and garnish with a shake of paprika.

Cream cheese and walnuts

Sandwich good shaped halved walnuts with cream cheese. You need approximately 2 oz. cream cheese to each 4 oz. halved walnuts.

Frankfurter and mustard rolls

Cut 4 slices of thin white or brown bread and butter. Spread with a thin layer of French mustard, then roll round a frankfurter sausage. Cut each roll into 4 portions.

Pâté and gherkin rolls

Cut 4–6 wafer-thin slices of brown bread and butter. Spread with liver pâté and put 1 or 2 well-drained gherkins on each slice of bread and butter. Roll, then cut into 4 slices and turn so that the green of the gherkin shows.

Pâté and asparagus rolls

Repeat as above, using 4 well-drained asparagus tips instead of gherkins.

Ham and asparagus rolls

These are made exactly the same way as above, but with wafer-thin slices of ham spread over the bread and butter, and rolled round asparagus tips.

Sardine pyramids

Hard-boil 2 eggs, shell, chop the whites and yolks separately. Mix the chopped egg white with a small can of well-drained sardines. Form into pyramid shapes on tiny rounds of bread and butter or crisp biscuits. Garnish with the egg yolk.

Stuffed dates

Stone good quality dates and fill with cream cheese. You need approximately 3 oz. cream cheese to 12–14 dates.

Stuffed prunes

Stone cooked or tenderised prunes. Fill the centres with:

a) cream cheese blended with chopped nuts.

b) liver pâté and a blanched almond,

c) crisply fried bacon cut into snippets and blended with demi-sel cheese.

Haddock pyramids

Mince or flake 4 oz. cooked haddock very finely, mixing with mayonnaise and sieved white of hard-boiled egg. Season well, then form into pyramids on toast or biscuits and decorate with a ring of gherkins or olives.

Rectifying mistakes

If in spite of care the cooking is not very satisfactory it may be possible to remedy this before serving, e.g.

Lumpy sauces : take a flat whisk and whisk very hard indeed – while the sauce is still boiling. Very often the lumps come out – if not then rub the sauce through a sieve or put into a blender, switch on until smooth, and reheat.
Note : Never allow sauces with egg to boil when reheating or cooking.

Curdled mixtures : i.e. in an egg sauce or custard, whisk as above, removing pan from heat – if unsuccessful, sieve, add another beaten egg and cook again *without boiling*. When making cakes, if the fat and sugar curdles as the egg is added stir in a little flour until smooth again.

Burned flavour : if a soup, stew, etc. burns, *do not stir*, otherwise you mix the burned base with the rest of the mixture. Tip into a fresh pan. Taste the mixture, if there is a slight flavour of burned food add extra seasoning, a pinch of curry powder, or a little Worcestershire sauce.

Put burned pan to soak with a handful of salt. After soaking for a while bring slowly to the boil – most of the burned food will come away, enabling you to clean the pan with a nylon pan scourer or steel wool.

Too salty a flavour : if you taste vegetables and they appear to have been over-salted, heat fresh *unsalted* water in another pan. Strain the vegetables and cook for 1–2 minutes in the fresh water.

If potatoes have been cooked with too much salt, cream them, adding plenty of milk and a beaten egg or egg yolk, which absorbs the extra salt.

If a stew or soup has been oversalted either add a little Worcestershire sauce to give a 'bite', or milk for creamy flavour, or cook 1 or 2 potatoes in stew or soup to absorb surplus salt; the potatoes need not be completely cooked, allow about 10 minutes.

Not quite cooked : if when the meal is ready to serve the joint is not quite cooked due to faulty timing – and everything else is ready – slice the joint and heat on flat oven-proof dish for a few minutes, or put under a hot grill, or heat the slices in the gravy or sauce.

Index